Reason and teaching

Reason and teaching

Israel Scheffler

The Bobbs-Merrill Company, Inc.
Publishers, Indianapolis and New York

First published 1973
by Routledge & Kegan Paul Ltd

London

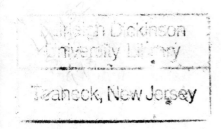
This edition published 1973
by The Bobbs-Merrill Company, Inc.
Copyright © 1973 by Israel Scheffler
Printed in the United States of America
No part of this book may be reproduced in
any form without permission from the
publisher, except for the quotation of brief
passages in criticism
Library of Congress Catalog Card Number 72–86641
ISBN 0–672–61253–4 (pbk)
ISBN 0–672–51854–6
First Printing

In memory of my mother

Ethel Scheffler
1883–1969

Contents

Contents

General editor's note

There is a growing interest in philosophy of education amongst students of philosophy as well as amongst those who are more specifically and practically concerned with educational problems. Philosophers, of course, from the time of Plato onwards, have taken an interest in education and have dealt with education in the context of wider concerns about knowledge and the good life. But it is only quite recently in this country that philosophy of education has come to be conceived of as a specific branch of philosophy like the philosophy of science or political philosophy.

To call philosophy of education a specific branch of philosophy is not, however, to suggest that it is a distinct branch in the sense that it could exist apart from established branches of philosophy such as epistemology, ethics, and philosophy of mind. It would be more appropriate to conceive of it as drawing on established branches of philosophy and bringing them together in ways which are relevant to educational issues. In this respect the analogy with political philosophy would be a good one. Thus use can often be made of work that already exists in philosophy. In tackling, for instance, issues such as the rights of parents and children, punishment in schools, and the authority of the teacher, it is possible to draw on and develop work already done by philosophers on 'rights', 'punishment', and 'authority'. In other cases, however, no systematic work exists in the relevant branches of philosophy—e.g. on concepts such as 'education', 'teaching', 'learning', indoctrination'. So philosophers of education have had to break new ground—in these cases in the philosophy of mind. Work on educational issues can also bring to life and throw new light on long-standing problems in philosophy. Concentration, for instance, on the particular predicament of children can throw new light on problems of punishment and responsibility. G. E. Moore's old worries about what sorts of things are good in themselves can be brought to life by urgent questions about the justification of the curriculum in schools.

There is a danger in philosophy of education, as in any other applied field, of polarization to one of two extremes. The work could be practically relevant but philosophically feeble; or it could be philosophically sophisticated but remote from practical problems. The aim of the new International Library of the Philosophy of Education is to build up a body of fundamental work in this area which is both practically relevant and philosophically competent. For unless it achieves both types of objective it will fail to satisfy those for whom it is intended and fall short of the conception of philosophy of education which the International Library is meant to embody.

R.S.P.

Acknowledgments

We wish to thank the authors, editors and publishers for their kind permission to reprint material previously published in their books or journals. Full details of the sources are given at the beginning of each essay.

Introduction

This book rests on the conviction that critical thought is of the first importance in the conception and organization of educational activities. Addressed to a variety of issues in the philosophy of education, it stresses the ideal of rationality as a unifying perspective relating theory and practice, moral and intellectual schooling, general studies and teacher education, the continuity and scope of the human heritage and the independent judgment and fresh vision which constitute our best hope for the future.

Written in an analytical spirit, the book ranges beyond self-imposed limitations that have often characterized professional work in recent educational philosophy. I have for several years advocated the analytical treatment of educational topics and the linking of general philosophical interests with the special concerns of education. But I have never construed analysis as a self-sufficient philosophical endeavor capable of yielding an independent school of educational thought. Analysis is indispensable to philosophy, but it requires material to work on and with. Philosophical treatment of educational themes indeed presupposes analytical tools and conceptions, but it addresses itself to our common world of knowledge and practice. The present book will, I hope, further underscore my belief that to separate thought from practice is detrimental to both, whereas to bring thought into communication with practice is to enrich the former and to illuminate the latter.

Educational practice, I am convinced, profits from the philosophical effort to crystallize and examine its basic concepts and guiding assumptions, while the scope of philosophical understanding is thereby enlarged. A corollary of this conviction is that a full and free exchange should characterize the relation between philosophy and educational theory. Educational practice should not be segregated from philosophical considerations, but this does not mean that its principles are to be derived from a superior philosophical vision; philosophy does not itself yield practical directives but it does not follow that it is therefore irrelevant to practice. Philosophy must learn from, as well as help to refine, practice; practice must inform theory but must, in turn, be qualified by theoretical reflection.

Nor is philosophy to be thought of as isolated from other studies bearing on educational practice. It is, to a large degree, in a 'second-order' position with respect to these other studies, concerned primarily, as it is, with their conceptual and methodological foundations. But its 'second-order' status implies neither superiority nor precedence; philosophy must respect the very studies that it aims to analyze, interpret, and criticize. And educational theory must, of course, draw upon the 'first-order' substantive materials available to it, as well as upon the critical analyses and interpretations of these materials which are the main fruits of philosophical concerns. Educational thought and teacher preparation ought, I believe, to be related to the whole family of studies which, in their most developed form, are represented in the university. This plurality of studies needs, as a whole, to be brought to bear on the critically important practices by which we rear our young and engage them in valued forms of thought and culture.

What unites the several studies is not a special method or technique but a common striving to develop forms of critical understanding, to define and progressively test criteria of rational judgment and associated principles of generalization and evaluation. This striving is embodied in the several traditions of thought, each providing a realization of the associated concepts of 'reason' and 'principle' within its sphere. To become rational is to enter into these traditions, to inherit them and to learn to participate in the never-ending work of testing, expanding, and altering them for the better.

Teachers, who are central to this fundamental process of human renewal, cannot be construed as mere classroom performers or agents of a policy laid down by others. They need to have entered sufficiently into the rational life themselves to be able to help the young also to enter. This requires that they be broadly educated, that they have a grasp of underlying principles and critical methods in their own fields, as well as a sense of the whole within which their fields may be located; it requires that they appreciate fundamental concepts and alternatives, and are thereby enabled to develop their own free judgment and sense of intellectual autonomy.

Teaching, construed along consonant lines, is not mere behavior modification. It is a human exchange, in which the role of reasons is paramount, in which the mutual climate of rational discussion tests the principles of the elders while it transfers to the young the very heritage founded upon these principles. Teaching is thus not a matter of shaping the young to preconceived specifications held immune to criticism. In teaching, the teacher reveals his reasons as well as his conclusions, thus inviting independent judgment of their persuasiveness and opening himself to the prospect of learning from the exchange. The word 'reason' in the title of this book is not meant to refer to some general faculty of the mind; it is to be understood throughout these discussions as always in the plural, referring in every case to the mutual sharing of reasons that I take to be central to teaching.

The essays collected here span seventeen years. The earliest of them was published in 1954 and the last was completed toward the end of 1971. Since four of them are new and the rest are scattered through a variety of publications that are rather difficult to assemble, the present book will, I hope, serve a useful purpose in collecting these formulations on related themes. Each essay was written for a particular occasion, prompted by the need to respond to a problem that seemed peculiarly pressing at the time of composition; as a whole, moreover, the essays lie within a period of unusual stress and change in our educational history. Nevertheless, I believe the several papers will be found to express a variety of unifying emphases despite the fact that they do not spell out a philosophical system. Some of these emphases have already been noted in the foregoing paragraphs, and further continuities will be evident from my account of the organization of the essays.

Despite their thematic and philosophical affinities, these papers display certain inevitable differences in tone and detail. To have attempted to eliminate all such variation by recasting the essays in line with present inclination would have meant destroying the originals in favor of a new treatise. While the present book is admittedly no substitute for such a treatise, it has, I believe, its own distinctive usefulness: it collects original statements in which there has been continuing interest, and it exhibits the interplay of philosophical analysis with the variable context to which it responds. I have accordingly edited very lightly, and have accepted the risk of straining the reader's indulgence through occasional stylistic variability or redundancy. In mitigation of this risk, I have included in the acknowledgments the year of publication or composition of each essay and indicated the source, or occasion of its presentation, to provide a sense of its context.

The period during which these essays originated is one in which I have also published several books on related topics. More systematic discussions of certain educational themes appear in *The Language of Education* and *Conditions of Knowledge*; aspects of the philosophy of science dealt with in *The Anatomy of Inquiry* and *Science and Subjectivity* also bear, in certain respects, on some issues treated here. Various of my editorial comments in *Philosophy and Education* (1958, 1966) deal with particular concepts of education and especially with the status of philosophy of education. *The Graduate Study of Education*, a report of a Harvard committee of which I served as chairman, outlines a viewpoint on the study of education within a university. The present book, addressed to a variety of educational issues, complements the treatment in these other works. It neither repeats what they have to say, nor is it dependent upon them, treating each of its topics afresh.

The analyses and interpretations it offers will, I hope, be of interest not only to educational theorists and philosophers but also to thoughtful educators and to the reflective general reader. Though its method and approach are philosophical, in a broad sense of that word, it presupposes no technical background in philosophy. Its intent, as a philosophical work, is to persuade only through critical means; the essays are to be taken not as certainties but as provisional formulations subject, in principle, to test by further reflection and argumentation. I hope the reader will concur that the problems treated are significant and the considerations adduced are relevant. He will, no doubt, judge for himself whether or not my reasoning and conclusions are sound. If he differs from me in the end, I will be glad if my book provides him with the occasion to advance his own critical thinking on the problems of education.

The book is organized into four parts. Part 1 is metaphilosophical; it is addressed to the status and prospects of philosophy of education. The initial essay, the earliest in the collection, is a call for the application and development of analytic methods in the treatment of conceptual issues in education. The second and third are recent, dealing, respectively, with the challenge to philosophy of the new activism, and with the opportunities for relating 'philosophies of' (e.g., philosophy of science, philosophy of history, philosophy of art, etc.) to curriculum conceptions and to teacher preparation. Part 1, as a whole, illustrates my belief that philosophy has an indispensable role in educational thought, a role that requires it to be at once critical and practical—linked to its general and historical preoccupations and pointed, at the same time, toward the analysis of ideas underlying educational practices.

Part 2 deals with general issues in the philosophy of education, addressing itself mainly to three questions: (i) Is the study of education to be conceived as a theoretical discipline? (ii) According to what philosophical model is teaching best interpreted? (iii) How is the education of teachers to be related to the scholarly studies represented in the university? These questions are, of course, interrelated, since conceptions of the study of education and the proper interpretation of teaching are likely to qualify preferred approaches to teacher education. Moreover, consideration of the teacher's role is itself likely to bear on the interpretation of education as a field of study as well as on the conception formed of teacher preparation. Part 2 adopts a pluralistic attitude: rejecting the notion of education as a theoretical discipline, it takes the study of education to focus rather on questions of practice, to which a variety of disciplines are relevant. Teaching is itself interpreted pluralistically: employing information but concerned with stimulating insight; developing principles of action and judgment but appealing always to the critical understanding of underlying reasons. The university setting, ideally, encourages teacher education to draw upon the plurality of studies capable of illuminating educational practice; it also locates the teacher's work within a broad array of theoretical viewpoints and critical alternatives, thus enhancing his rational understanding and his independent judgment.

Part 3 is concerned with educational content, that is, with questions of curriculum. How, for example, are decisions affecting the curriculum to be judged? What relations are there between science education and moral education, between morality and the democratic ideal, between theory and practice, between the content of schooling and the needs of society? Part 3 takes questions of content to be fundamental and, indeed, inescapable for education; moreover, they cannot be answered by reference to psychological, sociological, and organizational factors alone. Drawing upon philosophical interpretations of various content areas, Part 3 addresses itself to these questions, criticizing, in passing, certain prevalent conceptions of science, morality, and theory as ingredients of education. The concept of rational criticism, already discussed in earlier parts, is here emphasized as a link between the spheres of science, moral judgment, and the democratic ideal; it is also interpreted (following a similar emphasis in the second essay of Part 1) as a fundamental element of individual autonomy. It is worth noting that the final essay of Part 1 is closely related to the concerns of Part 3, suggesting the relevance of philosophy to curriculum thinking in a manner illustrated by various discussions in the latter part.

Part 4 presents critical interpretations of the work of five thinkers whose writings deal with matters of basic interest to education. These writings, representing a variety of philosophical tendencies, center on three main themes: (i) the nature of knowledge and thinking, (ii) the relation of theory to practice, and (iii) the role of philosophical thought. Each of these themes has already been introduced in earlier parts: the first in essays 6 and 10, the second in essays 4, 7, 8, and 10, and the last in Part 1. The essays of Part 4 offer, however, independent discussions that add considerably to the earlier treatments, and serve as well to introduce detailed consideration of the work of important writers. A substantially new emphasis, anticipated by a brief treatment in essay 6, is represented by the critique of behavioristic notions in essays 14 and 15. The concluding essay draws together the main themes of earlier parts in its concern with practical thought as a focus for curriculum, with the relations among the theoretical disciplines, with the role of philosophy, and with conceptions of teacher education. Part 4 offers, then, in the context of a critique of important writings, a further exploration of central issues of educational content and educational thought.

It is impossible for me to list all those from whom I have learned during the long period in which these essays originated; a small part of my indebtedness, at any rate, will be revealed by notes to the several papers. For the rest, a general acknowledgment to teachers, colleagues, and students must suffice. I wish, however, to express here my thanks to Professors Jane Martin and Michael Martin for helpful advice, and to Professor Frederick A. Olafson for critical remarks on several of the essays. To Samuel Scheffler I am indebted for preparation of the index.

I appreciate the support of the John Simon Guggenheim Memorial Foundation and the Center for Advanced Study in the Behavioral Sciences during the final stage of preparation of this book.

Israel Scheffler
Stanford, California

Philosophy and education

Toward an analytic philosophy of education

I

Various activities may, with historical justification, lay claim to the honored title of 'philosophy.' These include, among others, e.g., logical analysis, speculative construction, culture criticism, institutional programming, and the expression of personal attitudes toward the world. It is my purpose neither to cast doubt on any of these claims nor to deny the appropriateness of any of these activities. I do, however, wish to stress the ambiguity of the general term 'philosophy' and, correlatively, of the narrower term 'philosophy of education.' It is certainly no striking news that the latter term is currently widely employed to mean practically anything from a well-articulated metaphysics of knowledge to the vaguest expression of attitudes toward, say, the public school system. What *is* worthy of note is that one legitimate meaning is almost consistently ignored: philosophy of education is rarely, if ever, construed as the rigorous logical analysis of key concepts related to the practice of education. In this paper, arguing for the fruitfulness of such an approach, I shall try, *first*, to explain and illustrate the general notion of philosophy as logical analysis, and *second*, to outline the ways in which logical analysis appears to me relevant to educational problems.

The conception of philosophy as the attempt to clarify key concepts is hardly a modern invention. For the attempt, by dialectical methods, to clarify the meaning of basic notions is at least as old as Socrates. What distinguishes current analysis is, first, its greater sophistication as regards language, and the interpenetration of language and inquiry, second, its attempt to follow the modern example of the sciences in empirical spirit, in rigor, in attention to detail, in respect for alternatives, and in objectivity of method, and third, its use of techniques of symbolic logic brought to full development only in the last fifty years. The result has been revolutionary for philosophic practice. New insights have been achieved in almost every area of traditional

Presented at a meeting of Section Q, American Association for the Advancement of Science, December 1953, and published in the *Harvard Educational Review*, Vol. 24 (1954), 223-30 (Copyright 1954 by President and Fellows of Harvard College).

philosophy. The individualism so characteristic of its past has, to a marked extent, been tempered by a sense of community of investigation, unified by method rather than doctrine, and by a common search for clarity on fundamental issues. That this development represents no mere doctrinal school is evident from the fact that it comprises sharp differences of opinion within itself, as well as from the fact that a number of its early formulations have undergone orderly revision under the pressure of criticism and new discoveries. Nor can such development be considered entirely negative, for progress has been made in the settling of some older problems and the recasting of new ones, progress that is widely acknowledged by students in this domain. It is, then, this union of scientific spirit and logical method applied toward the clarification of basic ideas that characterizes current analytic philosophy.

Since critical precision rather than doctrine is the essence of such philosophy, its significance is best conveyed by an examination of concrete instances. My first illustration to this purpose is drawn from the theory of meaning, with which current analysts are perhaps predominantly concerned, and in which some of the best work has been done. I must ask you, despite its abstractness and unfamiliarity, to consider it with me in some detail, since for this philosophy detailed precision is all. Yet, I hope such consideration will afford an insight into *general* method and approach, which may emerge even more sharply against an abstract and unfamiliar setting. At a later point, of course, I shall want to suggest educational applications. Meanwhile, it will perhaps be instructive to note how difficult is the attempt to avoid confusion even in a realm removed from the urgencies of practice, and how, even here, increasingly radical departures from common assumptions are necessitated by the quest for clarity.

Consider, then, the notions of meaning and existence. Two common assumptions about these notions are: (i) The meaningfulness of a sentence containing a singular term (i.e., a name, or descriptive phrase purporting to name a single entity) presupposes that this term actually *does* name, that is, that *there really exists* the entity purportedly referred to; failure to name removes the object of discourse and renders both the empty singular term and its context meaningless. (ii) The existence-commitments of a theory, i.e., the entities that must exist for it to be true, are revealed by the set of singular terms that it employs. Both assumptions turn out, upon analysis, exceedingly troublesome if we want to construct a consistent and fruitful account of meaning. Let us see why this is so.

Take, for example, a definite singular descriptive phrase of the form 'the such-and-such' as it appears in the sentence, 'The American President in 1953 plays golf.' No difficulty here. The descriptive phrase, we would ordinarily say, following (i), *names* some unique entity, Mr Eisenhower, while the sentence is a *meaningful* statement about this entity, asserting something true of it. The negation of this sentence, though false, we would declare still meaningful, as concerning the same single entity, named by the descriptive phrase in question.

Consider, now, the new sentence, 'The American Emperor in 1953 plays chess,' and its negation, 'It is not the case that the American Emperor in 1953 plays chess.' Now there is, in point of fact, no entity denoted by the descriptive phrase shared by both these sentences, i.e., 'The American Emperor in 1953.' It plainly does us no good to declare the first sentence false, since false sentences are meaningful anyway and such a declaration would violate (i). Further, if the first sentence is false, its negation must be true, under the very same condition of failure to name by the identical descriptive phrase. So that a simple resolution to abandon (i) by taking failure to name as always implying falsity turns out to be impossible.

To hold on to (i) in the face of these two sentences, we must declare them both meaningless. But the consequences of such a course are plainly undesirable on two basic counts: first, it would hinge the very meaning of descriptive phrases inconveniently on fact. In general, we should prefer to keep the meaningfulness of our language independent of specific factual considerations; we want to consider our hypotheses meaningful even prior to any factual confirmation. Following the last proposal, however, we should require factual evidence of the existence and uniqueness of some appropriate named entity before we could even be confident we were *making sense* in using descriptive phrases, let alone asserting a truth by their use. Second, and perhaps more paradoxically, to make meaninglessness a consequence of failure to name, as our last proposal does for the two sentences under consideration, means that we cannot, within our language, even *deny* the existence of the American Emperor in 1953. For to do so, we should need to say something like, 'The American Emperor in 1953 does not exist,' and this sentence itself turns out, by our last proposal, to be strictly meaningless.

An analogous problem arises for proper names. Suppose I deny that Zeus exists. A fairly reasonable position. Yet consider: if, in using proper names, I make sense only by talking *about* some actual entity, following (i), what in the world am I talking *about* in saying 'Zeus does not exist'? In order for me to make sense, Zeus must exist, but if he does, my denial is false. Must I therefore admit, out of logical necessity, the existence of all members of the Pantheon, all characters in fiction, in short everything bearing an ostensible proper name? Furthermore, taking my denial statement as a miniature theory with one proper name ('Zeus'), it is clearly intended that, contrary to (ii), this name should be no clue to its existence-commitments, for it is intended to stand plainly committed to nothing, and certainly not to Zeus.

A well-known, and by now classic solution of the puzzle of descriptive phrases, which, in effect, abandons assumption (i) altogether for such phrases, was proposed many years ago by Bertrand Russell.[1] Briefly, Russell showed how to *eliminate* descriptive phrases in context, in favor of equivalent contexts no longer containing any phrases purporting to name unique entities, but referring quite generally to entities by means of logical variables like 'something,' 'nothing,' 'everything,' etc. Such elimination of contained descriptive phrases together with conservation of asserted content in effect divorces the contextual meaning from the purported naming function of such phrases altogether. For example, Russell's equivalent for our troublesome first sentence above is, 'Something is an American Emperor in 1953 and plays chess and nothing else is an American Emperor in 1953.' Though as a whole equivalent to the original, this translation provides no naming unit as a counterpart to the eliminated descriptive phrase. With this, the whole original problem disappears, there now being no difficulty in declaring this equivalent false, together with the original. But the upshot is the denial of (i) for descriptive phrases, since the original sentence is now construed as false (and its negation as true), hence perfectly meaningful, though the contained descriptive phrase fails to name. A corollary is denial of (ii) for descriptive phrases, since, if they can be significantly used without naming, they are no clue to the existential presuppositions of the theory.

A solution of the proper name puzzle has been proposed by Professor W. V. Quine[2] who extends Russell's analysis by showing how all proper names may be construed as descriptive phrases and then eliminated as before. For our above example, we are counseled by Quine to construe, 'Zeus does not exist' as, 'The thing that is-Zeus does not exist,' Russell's equivalent of which becomes, 'Either for each entity, it is not the case that it is-Zeus or there is more than one entity which is-Zeus.' Again, since no proper name or descriptive phrase purporting to name a unique entity appears at all in this translation, there remains no difficulty in declaring it and its original meaningful, and moreover, true. One upshot is denial of (i) even where a purported *proper name* fails to name. Consequently, a second result is full denial of assumption (ii), since, for this analysis, proper names are clearly no better indicators of the existence-commitments of a theory than are its descriptive phrases, which are, for Russell, no indicators at all, as we have seen. As Quine's extension makes clear, existence-commitments are ultimately revealed solely by the use made of logical variables ('something,' 'each entity,' etc.) when the theory is put into Russellian form. But the details of this judgment are another story.

One further problem, taken from a more familiar area, will illustrate that analysis is capable of touching our most basic notions of practice to the quick. We all talk of confirming general hypotheses by gathering relevant instances. For example, we say that a purported general law is progressively confirmed or disconfirmed by observation of its relevant instances. But consider the puzzle noted by Professor Hempel.[3] What is a confirming instance for the purported law, 'All ravens are black'? Clearly a raven which is black. A non-raven we would classify as clearly irrelevant altogether. Now, however, consider that our law is logically equivalent to the statement, 'All non-black things are non-ravens,' and for this statement a confirming instance would be a non-black non-raven. But this instance we have decided was irrelevant to the first law. Shall we say that what is to be taken as an instance depends on the accident of linguistic formulation? Let us rather rule that logically equivalent sentences should be confirmed by exactly the same instances. This rule, however, is just as counter-intuitive as ever, since if a non-black non-raven is to confirm our first law, then every time I observe the sky, the sun, my typewriter, or Widener Library, I am progressively confirming the law that all ravens are black. Clearly our ordinary conceptions of what constitutes an instance are faulty somewhere, and require considerable refinement.

Enough now of general illustrations of analytic problems and methods. I have already intimated that analytic philosophers are by no means exclusively concerned with theory of meaning and philosophy of science. Indeed, much work in ethics, theory of mind, philosophy of law, aesthetics, and theory of social science is presently under way. It is time, I think, to consider how analytic philosophy might be brought to bear on educational problems, as a legitimate and vital pursuit of philosophy of education. In analogy with applications of science to education,

I suggest that we conceive of analytic applications in roughly two directions: (a) the utilization of results already achieved in the autonomous development of research, and (b) the use of acknowledged methods directly in the study of educational problems.

(a) To realize fully the extent to which the first mode of application is presently feasible, one would ideally require a detailed survey of current analysis which, as already noted, touches a wide variety of areas. To take one example from the theory of knowledge, we might consider for a moment the rather fashionable proposal of Dewey[4], Neurath[5], and others[6], to replace the venerable notion of truth by that of probability or verification, or analogous ideas, in view of the impossibility of complete confirmation of hypotheses. Despite its wide popularity, however, and despite the hasty conclusions drawn for practice, perhaps most analysts are agreed that such replacement would be an error, in view of Professor Tarski's[7] semantic conception of truth. For Tarski, to say that a given sentence, e.g., 'the sun is shining,' is true, is to say nothing more nor less than 'the sun is shining.' On the other hand, to say that the latter sentence is confirmed by John Doe to degree d at time t is obviously to make an independent assertion, since it may hold whether or not the sun is shining in point of fact, and vice versa. It follows that truth and confirmation are independent. As Professor Carnap[8] has pointed out, were the impossibility of complete confirmation to rule out the term 'is true,' it would equally rule out the term 'is shining' and, indeed, every scientific term, while if partial confirmation is sufficient for retention of a term, then the term 'true' is as acceptable as any. What is ruled out by the pervasiveness of probability is certainty, not truth.

An illustration, now, from the theory of value. It has been argued, at least since Aristotle, that the pattern of justifying beliefs relative to evidence implies that some beliefs must be certain. For if we justify some belief on evidence and this evidence on further evidence, where do we stop? We cannot continue to justify every belief relative to evidence without infinite regress. Hence, if any belief is justified, some must be known certain in themselves. Now this persuasive argument for rationalism, as shown by Professor Goodman,[9] is somewhat too extravagant. In order to avoid infinite regress, we need only hold some beliefs with some initial credibility. We need attribute certainty to none. While we try to attain and preserve a maximum of initial credibility for the total mass of our beliefs, any single one is subject to withdrawal under pressure of conflict with this total mass. Goodman's argument may, as I have suggested,[10] be extended to ethical justification generally. For it is very widely held that in order to justify any act, goal, or choice, some at least must be held absolutely immune to withdrawal. What we need admit, it seems to me, is only that some choices or goals may have for us some degree of initial committedness, while none is immune to withdrawal. Whereas no act or choice is justifiable in isolation, every act is subject to control by all in our attempt to harmonize them by maximizing initial committedness for the mass of our behavior. If this analysis is not mistaken, then both ethical absolutism and extreme subjectivism are avoided, a corollary with important bearings on value theory and education. The analysis of justification is presently being pursued from a variety of approaches[11] and may prove fruitful for problems in social theory, theory of democracy, and other areas related to education.

Since considerable attention has been given by analysts, not only to *general* problems in the theory of knowledge and the theory of value, but also to *foundation questions* of the several branches of our intellectual heritage (e.g., science, history, logic, mathematics, etc.), education may derive vital benefit from analysis in its concern with the strengthening and development of this heritage. For such strengthening and development inescapably involve operative conceptions of each branch, its basic perspectives and leading ideas, its main standards and methods of judgment. Critical analysis of foundations thus sharpens and enhances the operative conceptions that education employs.

(b) The second mode of application I mentioned above consists of the direct analysis of concepts related to the practice of education. What I have already said perhaps indicates the possibilities in this area better than any catalog I might offer. Yet it is worth noting at this point that, if obscurity surrounds such basic notions as 'existence,' 'truth,' and 'confirmation,' notions crucially employed and continually refined in the exact sciences, it may surely be expected to hamper the understanding of key notions tied to educational practice, notions like 'disposition,' 'experience,' 'skill,' 'achievement,' 'training,' 'intelligence,' 'character,' 'choice,' 'growth.' How shall we understand, to take but one example, the popular contention that growth is the goal of education? Clearly not every sort of growth is held desirable, witness growth in ignorance or brutality. Even if we eliminate obviously undesirable dispositions, shall we think of growth as simply the increase in dispositions acquired by the learner? This will not do, for a substantial part of growth consists in dropping off dispositions once mastered. We all at one time could shoot marbles pretty well but can do so no longer. Furthermore, in attempting a count of dispositions how shall we classify them? Is playing checkers one and playing chess another? If so, where do we put Chinese checkers? Finally, how shall we weight the progressive intensification of one disposition as against the multiplication of several?

Taking a new direction, we might, along lines reminiscent of Dewey, consider growth as the intensification of some master disposition, e.g., the ability to solve problems intelligently. But how is such intensification itself to be construed concretely? A simple increase in solved problems per unit time may not indicate growth if conjoined with a greater increase per unit time in perceived problems remaining unsolved. Shall we propose, then, as an appropriate indication of our meaning here, the ratio of solved problems to those perceived, per unit time? This would end in absurdity since, other things remaining equal, a decrease in perception would constitute growth, while an increase in sensitivity to problems would constitute regression. We might try a different move (as Dewey appears to in certain of his writings), and construe problems not as relative to the selectivity of a perceiver, but as somehow objectively built into the total situation. But such a move, while it is not obvious that it meets our original difficulties, clearly raises more troubles than we had to begin with: just what is a total situation, what kind of entities are objective problems, and how do we determine their character?

Now it is important not to confuse the import of my remarks here with the widespread demand for so-called operational definitions. If this were all that is involved, it would be quite easy to define growth operationally as increase in weight as measured in milligrams, or in height as measured in centimeters, or in the average number of hairs per square centimeter of scalp.[12] Such a course would have but one drawback, i.e., it would have nothing whatever to do with our original, predefinitional concept as it figures in the educational statement in question. What is required here, it seems to me, is not the application of operationalist slogans so much as a careful analysis or explication of our original concept, aimed at the distillation of a more precise counterpart, and finally, an examination of what consequences result for educational theory from rewriting it with such newly achieved precision, or possibly, from failure to attain additional clarity.

Nor do I here intend, by any means, to deny the possibility of a fruitful and significant clarification of the notion of growth as used in educational theory. I am pointing to what seems to me one genuine philosophic problem germane to education, calling for the use of analytic methods. And what I am urging generally is recognition of the need, by a rigorous and thorough application of such methods, to clarify the meaning of our basic educational ideas, as of all ideas we hold important. If philosophy of education accepts this task of clarification, it will be assuming not merely a familiar historical role, but one that is proving increasingly fruitful and stimulating in wide reaches of current philosophy, and that cannot fail to deepen our understanding of what we do when we educate.

Notes

1 *Introduction to Mathematical Philosophy*, 2nd ed., London: Allen & Unwin, 1920, Chap. XVI.
2 'On What There Is,' *Review of Metaphysics*, 2 (1948); and *From a Logical Point of View*, Cambridge: Harvard University Press, 1953.
3 C. G. Hempel, 'Studies in the Logic of Confirmation,' *Mind*, 54 (1945).
4 John Dewey, *Logic: the Theory of Inquiry*, New York: Holt, 1938.
5 O. Neurath, *Foundations of the Social Sciences*, Chicago: University of Chicago Press, 1944.
6 See F. Kaufmann, *Methodology of the Social Sciences*, Toronto: Oxford University Press, 1944.
7 A. Tarski, 'The Semantic Conception of Truth,' in H. Feigl and W. Sellars, eds, *Readings in Philosophical Analysis*, New York: Appleton-Century-Crofts, 1949.
8 R. Carnap, 'Truth and Confirmation,' in H. Feigl and W. Sellars, eds, *Readings in Philosophical Analysis*, New York: Appleton-Century-Crofts, 1949.
9 Nelson Goodman, *Problems and Projects*, Indianapolis: Bobbs-Merrill, 1972, pp. 60-8.
10 I. Scheffler, 'On Justification and Commitment,' *Journal of Philosophy*, Vol. LI (1954), 180-90.
11 See A. W. Burks and F. B. Fitch, 'Justification in Science,' in M. G. White, ed., *Academic Freedom, Logic, and Religion*, Philadelphia: University of Pennsylvania Press, 1953; H. Feigl, 'De Principiis Non Disputandum?', in M. Black, ed., *Philosophical Analysis*, Ithaca: Cornell University Press, 1950.
12 C. G. Hempel, *Fundamentals of Concept Formation in Empirical Science*, Chicago: University of Chicago Press, 1952. See the discussion of operationalism.

2   Philosophy of education and the new activism

The relation between philosophy and education

The philosophy of education has, paradoxically, not usually been conceived as a genuine branch of philosophy in our day. Although aspects of education occupied important, sometimes central, roles in the thinking of great ancient and modern philosophers, the subject has in recent times typically been organized and pursued as a primarily professional topic, largely cut off from the mainstream of general philosophical investigations.

The causes are complex and invite historical scrutiny. Certainly the general divorce of teacher training from liberal arts institutions seems to have played a role, and the fact that twentieth-century Anglo-American philosophy has been strongly oriented toward science and mathematics has been a further contributing factor. Yet the philosophy of law, the philosophy of art and the philosophy of religion have not, I believe, suffered equal isolation despite being subject to similar influences. Is the critical point that philosophy of education has been strongly claimed by the teacher training effort, whereas the corresponding claim has not been so strongly made in the training of lawyers, artists, and clerics? How then explain the lack of such a field as philosophy of medicine, equally unclaimed by medical schools and philosophy departments?

I do not, in any case, pretend to know the full answer, and would here merely commend the question to historians. I do, however, wish to declare my conviction that whatever the causes may be, the division itself between philosophy of education and general philosophy makes no sense. There is as much basis for philosophy of education, conceived as a genuine philosophical endeavor, as there is for philosophies of law, art, religion, history, science and mathematics. Each of these fields belongs within the main current of philosophical tradition, addressing itself, how-

Presented at a conference on 'New Directions in Philosophy of Education', sponsored by the Ontario Institute for Studies in Education, Spring 1970. It represents a response to new activistic trends in education generally, and in philosophy in particular.

ever, to a special realm of life as its primary domain.

As in the case of each of these fields, the proper relation between philosophy of education and its object realm is one of natural two-way communication. It is not for philosophy to dictate to fundamental areas of social and intellectual practice how they must carry out their work. The philosopher's job is not to deduce purported educational implications from his general doctrines any more than it is to derive purported legal, historical, or scientific implications. His task is to bring to bear philosophical methods, conceptions and traditions in seeking to understand the independent concerns of his object realm. Education, in particular, must be taken as seriously in its own right as science is taken by the philosophy of science. This does not mean that education must also be taken as fixed and unalterable, any more than science is so taken by philosophers of science. The relationship sought is a creative one—in learning from a genuine inquiry into education, philosophy's scope is extended and enriched; in striving for philosophical critique and perspective, education may attain a deeper and wider self-consciousness with inevitable bearings on practice.

Such a relation, it should be stressed, is not to be misconceived as a specific procedure or investigative approach. What is in question here is, broadly speaking, a region of philosophical work addressed to educational practice, and compatible with a wide variety of conceptual styles. No single program or paradigm of intellectual endeavor can be taken to exhaust the potentialities of philosophy of education as thus conceived. In particular, no school of thought, either of the traditional type or of the more recent analytic or existentialist varieties, ought properly to be identified with the philosophy of education as such. This does not, of course, mean that schools of thought are to be shunned. Schools and methodological programs are the lifeblood of thought; they provide direction and organization to the efforts of individual thinkers. What is in point here is pluralism within the region: the need and opportunity for a variety of programs and styles to flourish, all embraced within the continuous neighborhood relating philosophy and education.

Lest the envisaged pluralism seem to border on pure formlessness, however, the example of parallel fields may again be cited. Consider philosophy of science, for example: wide variation in problems, methods, focus, and intellectual approach prevails. Structural studies, conceptual analyses, naturalistic descriptions, normative reconstructions, historical approaches, and methodological investigations flourish. To be sure, the label 'philosophy' has its own magic, and there are some efforts carried on under its aegis that are very hard to construe as properly belonging with the above. Purely sociological, psychological, or political commentary, for example, or discussion of unsolved scientific problems are frequently called by the name. There is no point, moreover, in striving for exclusive ownership of the label. Nevertheless, it ought not to be supposed that the only conclusion is a virtual nihilism, for which anything at all is to be understood as philosophy, from an academic standpoint, which is willing thus to call itself. From the point of view of a concern with intellectual system and organization, only confusion can result from an attempt to bring all the heterogeneous items that may be designated 'philosophical' into a common category.

The issue is substantive, not verbal: what unifies the philosophical varieties I have in mind is primarily a concrete heritage of thought, embodied in shared writings focusing on common problems with shared rational aims, through commonly acknowledged forms of argumentation. Philosophers, in the sense I here intend, are those who by virtue of their training have become heirs to this heritage, have joined in its conversations spanning the centuries, have made themselves responsible for pursuing its questions under the intellectual circumstances of the present. They may, and do, exhibit great diversity in the execution of this responsibility, but they recognize in themselves reflections of a shared tradition perpetuated in common elements of training. If they address themselves to education, they take on special obligations: to take its ideas, assumptions, practices, history, and problems seriously and to test their philosophical endeavors, at least in part, by gauging their adequacy to educational phenomena independently appraised.

Nor should my talk of a creative relation between philosophy and education be taken to deny the so-called second-order character of philosophical endeavor. Philosophy, after all, takes education as its object of study. Let it be granted that educators themselves need to take a second-order stance respecting the teaching subjects in their curricular reflections, for example, and that they here may be said in turn to presuppose the philosophy of those subjects. Granted, in other words, that education is itself a two-level structure. Still, it falls to educational philosophy to assume a second-order attitude with respect to the whole of education, to take the whole structure as an object realm, striving to raise to critical consciousness its assumptions, orientations and modes of thought, and to deal with these using the resources of philosophical tradition. It does not claim any moral superiority by virtue of its second-order position, nor can it properly take any attitude other than respect for the phenomena which it is its purpose to study; yet it cannot without abdication deny its second-order status. Nor is the distinction here implied one of persons. Educators, like scientists, may themselves take on philosophical functions. In so doing they will be looking at their realms of practice from a second-order vantage point, and making contact with the body of philosophical tradition.

The philosophy of education as I conceive it, then, brings this concrete philosophical tradition into relation with the ideas, institutions and problems of educational practice. Basing itself upon the works constituting the corpus of such tradition, it must, equally, retain a live continuity with the efforts of those who now share this tradition and cope variously with the challenge to philosophize in the present. The isolation of the subject earlier referred to has been injurious precisely here—in cutting it off from continuing philosophical work in other realms, and thus from advances that accrue from the constant challenge of new ideas, methods, and questions.

Happily, the tide seems to me now to have turned, or at least to have begun to turn. In 1958, when I brought out the collection, *Philosophy and Education*, I devoted my introduction mainly to advocating an overcoming of the isolation above discussed, and to urging a fusion between philosophical rigor and educational concerns. In introducing the second edition of this book in 1966, I remarked that there had been considerable change in the situation during the intervening eight years. It seemed to me then that the rift between professional education and the arts and sciences generally had perceptibly narrowed and that academic scholars and researchers had begun to take education seriously as a field of investigation. I observed that the educational application of philosophical inquiries, in particular, had become more widespread and that there was now a 'recognizable and growing corpus of writings dealing relatively directly with educational matters in the spirit of general developments in philosophy...The important fact,' I concluded, 'is that the enterprise has clearly begun and is being carried forward, that the old walls are crumbling, and that a freer and friendlier communication between education and philosophy is being developed.' The task, it seemed to me then, was 'to move from possibilities and programs to substantive issues. What is primarily needed,' I said, was 'fresh constructive work on... concrete problems of educational thought.'

The challenge of the new activism

It is ironic, then, that after four years, I am here addressing myself to possibilities and programs once more, engaging in meta-philosophical discussion rather than concrete educational analysis. The occasion is, moreover, not a new situation affecting philosophy of education particularly, but a general re-orientation of attitude which seems to be arising in philosophy today, at any rate in the United States, and I suspect elsewhere. It is an alteration of mood and outlook, amounting perhaps to a crisis, certainly a crisis of self-confidence, facing the philosophical tradition generally, and bound therefore to have ramifications for philosophy of education in particular. It is further ironic that because philosophy of education has happily become closer to general philosophy, it has now become more vulnerable to the crisis affecting the latter. At any rate, it is this situation to which I wish to devote my remaining remarks.

What are the main features to be noted? There is, first of all, a new impatience with theoretical ideas, analysis, and argument; second, a growing rejection of the ideal of rationality; third, a revulsion from the demands of discipline and professional standards; and fourth, a tendency to reconstrue intellectual work as political ideology, continuous with political action. This is an impressionistic description of a climate and so, certainly, selective and subjective, but there is enough truth in it, I fear, to give us cause for serious reflection. I do not say that the attitudes described are now universal or even predominant, but rather that they are sufficiently visible among a growing segment of younger thinkers to warrant our concern.

For though the attitudes I have described are not, perhaps, in the first instance directed against philosophy in a deliberate way, they are directly opposed in fact to the whole spirit and direction of philosophy, past and present. Philosophy *is*, after all, theory based upon argument, as elaborate and as detailed as may be required to ascertain the truth of the matter, argument which follows no external lead but which itself leads those engaged in the quest for understanding. The whole concept of argument, moreover, rests upon the ideal of rationality—of discussion not in order to move or persuade, but rather to test assumptions critically by a review of *reasons* logically pertinent to them. The testing of such assumptions is not an easy task, nor the fruit of a skill inborn only in the fortunate. Philosophical ability is the product of learning and experience, in particular of intellectual contact with the recorded argumentation of past philosophers and with the best critical work of contemporary philosophers and logicians; it is an outgrowth of the discipline of philosophical training and is crystallized in professional standards of philosophical work. Finally, though philosophy is concerned with politics, it is also concerned with other realms of human experience, with ethics and history, with science and art, with religion and education, with mathematics and the mind. And its purpose is to find the truth and to achieve understanding, not to propagate partisan creeds or to engage in political action.

The growing general attitudes I have earlier described are thus set in opposition to the main tendencies of philosophy. In the degree to which these attitudes increasingly form the general habits of mind of our youth, philosophy is confronted, not merely with an internal dispute, but with an opposition across the generations. As these attitudes are specifically focused on philosophy as a subject, the latter is, in effect, faced with the demand that it redefine itself in ideological terms, make itself socially activistic, and transform itself into a militant agency of some program of political change. Having, after long effort and many struggles, emancipated itself, in certain countries at least, from the domination of state and church, it may now need to cope with the most poignant and difficult challenge of all— that of its own youth who would bend it to the service of what they see as a larger and more urgent cause than philosophical understanding. Socrates was accused by his fellow Athenians of corrupting the youth. Today, some of our youth accuse philosophy of corruption.

Abstract and remote, pretending to an objective standpoint beyond politics, bloodlessly rational and calculating, philosophy (they say) diverts energy from the imperative task of altering an utterly evil *status quo*. Blind to the human misery around it, it callously plays with words instead of helping to mobilize militant revolutionary sentiment and radical action. By such intellectual diversion, it helps in fact to rationalize and bolster existent evils and enters into complicity with them. Its vaunted rationality, like that of science, is in fact merely its capacity to shape men to the specifications of a repressive industrial society. The proper task of philosophy is thus to transform its traditional purposes and preoccupations, to cease its hair-splitting and logic-chopping, and enlist in the radical cause of social change through direct political action. Or, to alter the figure, it must cease to fiddle while the world burns; its morally self-evident duty is to join the fire brigade.

Reflections on the challenge

The circumstances and specific features of the charge may be new but the general aspects are all too familiar. The mention of Socrates recalls the fact that, from the earliest times, philosophy has been considered a threat to settled creeds and established social views, an affront both to practical men and to ideologues who would use it for their own designs, and thus destroy it. For there is no comparison between genuine philosophy and the efforts of thinkers in the service of a cause antecedently fixed. The call for a transformation of philosophy into militant activism is thus a call, not for a revised philosophy, but for a surrender of philosophy altogether. A philosophy subservient to a practical creed, a philosophy whose work is not argument but the mobilization of sentiment, whose goals are not open to discussion but are presumed self-evident, whose quest for critical understanding is belittled as hair-splitting and curtailed in the name of higher urgencies—this is a philosophy that is no philosophy at all. The charge is, then—let us be clear about it—that philosophy is abstract, callous, and compliant with evil—an obstacle to the revolutionary transformation of society; and the proposal is to do away with it, substituting militant activism for philosophical activity. It is, in any event, as utterly misleading to call such activism a new form of philosophy as it would be to call death a new form of life.

What are we to make of this proposal? Has the time come at long last for philosophy to die? Consider the analogy of music: abstract and remote, pretending to a standpoint beyond politics, it diverts energy from the imperative tasks of revolutionary change. Callously playing with notes in the midst of human misery, it in fact rationalizes the *status quo*; it must transform itself into an agency of radical social change. If this sounds far-fetched, recall that it is fiddling while Rome burns that provides a central metaphor for the basic orientations under attack. Recall, too, Plato's banishment of the poets, and his strict notions of musical education; recall, too, the vicious attempts in our own century to harness literature and the arts to political dogmas of party and state. Philosophy, scientific theory, literature, and the arts are, I suggest, in the same position in the relevant respects—they cannot be made subservient in principle to external direction, no matter how moral or politically urgent such direction is claimed to be, for they do in fact claim purposes beyond morality and beyond politics. A view that finds such neutrality repugnant cannot hope to save these pursuits while destroying their freedom; it must, further, to be consistent, be prepared to sacrifice them all for its partisan ends. Such a price is likely to be thought too high by all but the most extreme proponents of the partisanship in question.

A more moderate version of their charges may, however, be directed, not against the abstract pursuits in question, but against their practitioners. It will no longer be said, for example, that philosophy itself is to become a form of militant activism, but that philosophers are to devote themselves to such activism, not *qua* philosophers, but *qua* men. Philosophy, science, literature, and art are, on this account, acknowledged to be conceivable as pursuits beyond politics, but it is, in the present state of the world at least, immoral to engage in them. Fiddling is all right in itself, but the fiddler is reprehensible who fiddles when the world is aflame.

It must, to begin with, be admitted that there is an important element of truth in the line of thought just sketched. No pursuit, no matter how exalted, can claim absolute allegiance from its practitioners without diminishing their humanity. A philosopher, or scientist, or artist, who is responsive only to the demands of his calling, but not to the suffering of other human beings whose pain he might, through his efforts, alleviate, is not immune to criticism simply because his calling is beyond morality. For no man, as distinct from a pursuit or calling, is himself beyond morality. His work may fulfil the highest professional or artistic standards, and yet we may judge him to be morally unworthy as a person, or find that his actions had failed to satisfy relevant moral requirements. Moreover, the actions in question are not necessarily to be conceived to occupy a remote realm, neatly segregated from the area of the calling involved. For to pursue a calling is itself an action subject to broader moral considerations, and these considerations may in theory conflict with professional appraisal of the pursuit in question. If an artist, absorbed in his painting, ignores the illness of his infant child, who dies through his neglect, we shall judge his action immoral even though the painting turns out a masterpiece.

This example is certainly too simple for the general problem before us, but it serves to illuminate a general point: every person's actions, even those through which he devotes himself to his calling, remain subject to moral appraisal. There is no escape from the practitioner's moral predicament: his need to weigh the pursuit of his calling against alternative possible pursuits; to decide how much time, effort, and energy are to be given to his profession or art and how much to conflicting activities acknowledged to make legitimate moral demands upon him. Nor is this a routine or generalizable sort of decision to make. The alternatives are certainly not typically as clearcut as in the example given above, nor is there a general equality among practitioners with respect to their capacities to execute actions thought to have an independent moral sanction.

Now it must be admitted that there is great variation within each calling in the sensitivity of its practitioners to the predicament here outlined. It must further be conceded that each calling provides an ideal perspective of thought or value which tends, by its very powers of absorption, to draw a man away from the complex and imponderable questions of moral choice. Still, such choices *are* complex and imponderable at best; they are delicate and individual—they cannot without arrogance be subsumed under a general maxim and applied routinely to all practitioners of a calling. One would hope that our education and public discourse might encourage a general sensitivity to moral and social problems in all the members of society, but one would surely need to leave the particular decisions and continuing dilemmas to be dealt with by each person in his solitude. The call for philosophers, as men, to give up their professional pursuits and to turn, in a body, to a fixed program of militant activism presumes to answer the question in advance and in general for all philosophers; such arrogance cannot itself, I suggest, be judged moral.

Nor should it be overlooked that, though the appeal is here directed to philosophers rather than construed as a revision of philosophy, the effect of its fulfillment would nevertheless be likely to involve serious damage to its future prospects. Here the moderate version we are discussing merges with the more extreme attack against philosophy itself. Now it is in theory conceivable that one might judge it worth sacrificing or seriously damaging the prospects of philosophy in order to accomplish some end in given circumstances. But the circumstances would need to be extreme indeed to make such a judgment even hypothetically plausible. And the assessment of their extreme character would itself require a rational base in the evaluation of conditions and the consideration of alternative possibilities of action. Such a rational base, it may further be suggested, is more than likely to presuppose philosophical argument as a fundamental component.

To advocate some species of radical militancy on the basis of a particular assessment of social circumstances and *at the same time* to attack the very ideal of rational thought and theoretical analysis is therefore self-defeating, and cuts the ground from under the advocacy in question. Certainly there is no dearth of evils in the world; the horrible features and tragic prospects of human affairs on this planet in our day are visible to all who have eyes. Yet the call for revolutionary action, the particular social diagnoses, the pointed charges of hypocrisy, rationalization, and complicity, the advocacy of militant programs of radical change—these are not deductive consequences of the evils to be observed, nor are they self-evident. They rest, in each instance, on a quite specific set of interpretations and analyses of a moral, social and philosophical character, as well as on a set of strategic and tactical judgments as to what actions may have what effects, as a matter of empirical fact. The very basis of the proposals urged is thus a matter for scientific and philosophical —certainly for rational—assessment. If the latter are argued out of bounds for reasons of emergency, this basis can itself have no authority whatever.

A contemporary theologian once criticized philosophers for spending too much time debating God's existence, rather than affirming His attributes. Of course, to affirm His attributes is, at least provisionally, to grant His existence; simultaneously to renounce debate over His existence amounts therefore to adopting a positive answer without rational evaluation. To say, similarly, that rationality has preoccupied us too much, and that we now need forthwith to join the ranks of convinced militant activists working for some particular version of radical change is to counsel acceptance, without rational evaluation, of the philosophical and empirical underpinnings of such activism. It is to urge that we swallow the presupposed diagnosis in the manner of a theological premiss. The diagnosis requires argument; but then, in the nature of the case, it requires philosophy.

Can it not, then, be imagined that rational thought, generally, supports a diagnosis so extreme as to call for its own *subsequent* dissolution? In hypothetical cases this is perhaps conceivable, but it is difficult to imagine conditions so extreme in any factual circumstances likely to arise. For consider what is implied. Without rational thought, we can have no reason to suppose that our guiding beliefs are true and so trustworthy; we therefore can have no assurance that actions based upon such beliefs are warranted. To counsel a continuing program of radical action in a complex and changing world environment, while disparaging the future prospects of rational analysis, is therefore to advocate a long-term policy that is blind. One can conceive fantastic circumstances in which one might need to pluck out one's eyes in order to survive; but one would correspondingly need to anticipate with sorrow a severe reduction in capacity to explore the physical environment. To damage our rationality would be an even more desperate measure destructive of all capacity for intelligent orientation in the world. A confident commitment to an active program jettisoning rational thought is a counsel not only of blindness but of fanaticism. For if the philosopher is, as has been said, one who searches for an exit from a dark cave, with the aid of a tiny, flickering candle, the fanatic is he who blows out the candle, proclaiming, confidently, 'Follow me!'

Rationality has just been characterized as a precious instrument for assessing truth and for gauging the trustworthiness of courses of action. It must, however, also be conceived as an autonomous character trait. That is to say, it is not simply a tool used by a developed ego to solve its problems in the world, but enters, so to speak, into the very structure of the ego itself in so far as the ego is capable of identifying problems, formulating coherent choices, grasping propositions and maxims, and gauging their import for intended action. If rationality is an instrument, it can be regularly used only by those whose characters embody rational dispositions. We do not normally focus upon our own characters in analyzing specific problems of action in the environment, but we presuppose them nevertheless. If, employing our own rational resources, we embark on a program damaging to the prospects of rational character-building in the future, we project a social policy for persons who can hardly be conceived as sustaining any such policy, for they will lack the ego-structure required for any developed form of social life. Specialized rational pursuits such as science and philosophy and, for similar if not identical reasons, art and literature, are not to be conceived as solely instrumental. Yet it does not follow that they are therefore luxuries, to be easily sacrificed to other things when emergency threatens. For where they do not directly solve problems, they still help form the human problem-solver. To be capable of transcending the world of politics through philosophical reflection or literature or art or science is a fundamental achievement of human beings, nourishing those capacities that life requires, to be lived at a human level. There is then, paradoxically, a certain point to fiddling in a world aflame—consider, for example, the fiddler on the roof.

Does it follow, then, that we are doomed to quietism? Is radical action to be generally shunned? Are all activist programs to be eliminated so that we may sit in our studies and speculate? These questions are, or at least should be seen as, absurd on their face. For they reflect an ancient, and false, conception of reason and action as dwelling in separate realms. If one reasons, according to this conception, one does so with the mind and does not thereby act, for action is of the body. If one acts, one employs the body and does not in such employment reason, for reason is of the mind. Reason paralyzes action, for the person can be occupied in one or the other but not in both together.

This is not the place for a critical discussion of the conception cited nor for a sermon on the continuities of thought and action. It suffices to say that reason is not a realm, *a fortiori* not a realm separate from action. Nor, though it gives rise to such specialized ideal pursuits as science and philosophy, is it to be *identified* with any of them, for the practitioner's moral predicament earlier discussed, which pits such pursuits against alternative activities, is itself subject to rational critique. Reason is rather a matter of continuing responsibility for evaluation, by logically pertinent reasons, of the credentials of beliefs and choices. Reason is therefore not opposed to action, even radical action; it is opposed to *fanaticism*, i.e., the rigid adherence to doctrines without a willingness to take responsibility for their logical critique by relevant evidence and alternative views. To reject fanaticism is not to reject action. It is dangerous nonsense to suppose that only the impotent can reason and only the fanatics can act. The problem for each of us is to choose social action rationally, to decide how much and what sort of effort to invest in it, to continue to monitor the consequences of our own commitments, and to try, despite the difficulties and traumas of the present, and despite reluctant curtailments required by emergency, to maintain those common links with universal pursuits such as art, literature, and philosophy, without which our future is not likely to be human no matter how successful our programs.

As for philosophy of education, I will not say much specific to it here. My anticipation is that theoretical, critical, and analytical pursuits will come increasingly under attack from dogmatic activism here as elsewhere. Educators are perhaps better prepared than others to spot some of the characteristic attitudes we have discussed, for they have seen analogues relating to the school. They have known those educational doctrines for which the school is an instrument to be harnessed to some fixed social scheme, for which the school cannot be neutral and for which its rational, as distinct from its political, content is a mere hypocritical pretense. And they realize, too, that such doctrines are themselves ingenious ideologies in support of views pretending to be above criticism. Educators are also inclined to realize the worth of critical ideas, for they know that these ideas form the essential human context within which any problems must be faced. They are not, one hopes, easily converted to anti-intellectualistic dogmatisms.

At any rate, I trust my belief will by now be evident that philosophy of education is in itself, and as a theoretical pursuit, an important and legitimate activity, which we must—no matter how desperate the world seems to become, and no matter how we individually allocate our energies to alternative demands—strive to reserve a place in our minds for, not only as a primary component of rational educational decision but as a humanizing sustenance of the spirit, if the spirit survives.

Philosophy
and the curriculum

3

Long conceived as primarily a professional subject, the philosophy of education has in recent years been developing closer
ties with general philosophy. The latter, meanwhile, has grown
increasingly aware of the significance of education as an area of
reflection and inquiry. This *rapprochement* has created new
opportunities but also new problems: how, fundamentally, to
bring philosophical thought to bear significantly on educational
practice? Many of us have for a long time been critical of the
old gulf between general philosophy and philosophy of education; we have also attacked the inspirational role of the latter in
teacher training and its presentation in stale typological categories that could only seem artificial in the context of the general
development of our subject. Yet the old way must be conceded
to have had its advantages. Though cut off from the philosophical
mainstream, it was at least acknowledged on all sides as having
a legitimate place in teacher training. Though oversimplified
and often naïve in conception, it at least addressed issues recognizable to the practitioner. Though frequently artificial in
structure and treatment, it at least provided an identifiable traditional framework for course development by those assigned to
teach it.

What have we, the critics, proposed to put in its place? We
have urged a desegregation process, a closer connection between
general and educational philosophy, in the interests of an en-
richment of the former and a sounder and more sophisticated
development of the latter. These motivations were, and I
believe, continue to be, worthwhile. They provide challenging
options for beneficial intellectual innovation in a variety of
directions. Yet the very diversity of possibilities has created a
diffuseness of purpose, a hesitancy or ambivalence as to the roads
to be taken. The departure from tradition has exacted the usual

Presented at the Working Conference in the Philosophy of Education
sponsored by the Council for Philosophical Studies, February 1971.
A preliminary version was presented at a meeting of the Center for
Philosophic Exchange of the State University of New York at Brock-
port, Fall 1970.

penalty of unsettled directions, amorphous and confused strivings, threatening freedom. Moreover, in bringing educational philosophy nearer the condition of general philosophy, the desegregation process has produced a new remoteness by comparison with the older tradition. Attention has, naturally, tended to focus increasingly on issues of general interest, and the largely analytical cast of contemporary philosophy has, moreover, invited an increasingly detailed and theoretical development of issues in place of a largely practical orientation. With the best will in the world, educational philosophers have been drawn into the delights of the maze, and the road back has seemed harder and harder to find. Without a clear channel of address to questions of the practitioner, the role of educational philosophy in teacher training has become more obscure.

No one supposes, to be sure, that the philosopher's task is practical engineering or applied science. And it should certainly be insisted that the quest for philosophical insight is generally long and circuitous, ranging far beyond local arrangements and predicaments. Yet the *linkage* of philosophical and practical concerns must nevertheless be maintained; the *continuity* of theoretical understanding and the questions of practice must still be affirmed. Even the critics aimed, after all, at a desegregation of fields, and desegregation is not achieved by swallowing one field whole. The challenge is to create a genuine communication between the methods and ideas of current philosophical work and the concerns and categories of learning and schooling. The aim is, to be sure, philosophical understanding, at the *level* achievable in contemporary inquiry generally, but the *object* of such understanding remains the educational process.

Nor should it be supposed that the current difficulties of *rapprochement* that we have been describing could somehow have been avoided by a formula, that their very existence therefore testifies to human error or blindness. On the contrary, it seems to me that such a *rapprochement* between fields is a genuinely open affair, in which the range of potentialities cannot possibly be foreseen and in which a period of exploration and experimentation is rather to be anticipated. The old barriers were, after all, limiting—they channeled intellectual effort into a relatively small set of fixed directions. Like social segregation, they provided a structured system hampering the fullest communication between separated segments. Elimination of such hampering conditions does not, in itself, provide new and richer channels; it merely sets the stage for their discovery or invention. Such discovery and invention are not automatic products of some magical routine. They depend upon exploration of objective possibilities in an experimental frame of mind. There is risk in such experimentation and there are no guaranteed successes. But there is also no turning back to the false security of limited perspectives. The opportunities need to be tried, the many pathways explored, in a pluralistic and scientific spirit. If there is current unsettlement, there is also the promise of new ideas and new understanding to be gained. To bring the rich heritage and contemporary sophistication of philosophy into significant relation with the multiple concerns of education represents a high challenge to creative effort.

It is my conviction that no single program ought to dominate in such effort. There are many things that need doing. Continuity is not the same thing as uniformity. It is perfectly compatible with a pluralism of programs and aims; what it requires is only that there be connecting paths available for those who would travel from theory to practice and back again. These paths may themselves be diverse; there are footpaths and highways, difficult mountain passes, sea-lanes and jet routes. Nor is the construction of a given path the work of one man or program. Work in cultivating an isolated area may become significant through the forging by others of a remote, though vital, link. The last completed link makes the chain, but its significance depends on the availability of all the others. In the linking of philosophy and education there are numerous directions to be explored—promising routes, for example, between moral philosophy and studies of character development, between epistemology and cognitive psychology, between social philosophy and the setting of educational aims, to name but three. In outlining the specific attractions of philosophies-of in the remainder of my paper, I would thus by no means be understood as denying the claims of other possibilities. Rather, my aim is to develop the indications of promise that seem to me to point in one given direction, in the hope that this direction at least will receive some attention. For though many routes are possible, a mere contemplation of their several potentialities will in itself make no new pathways. My suggestion is that we have, at least here, a worthwhile place for constructive work—work that promises, moreover, to link philosophy with educational practice in a concrete and articulate manner.

I was first led to this suggestion several years ago, through teaching certain introductory philosophy of education courses to prospective teachers, and perhaps I may therefore be pardoned for calling upon my personal experience to explain the appeal of the idea. The central themes of these courses were taken from epistemology, and touched on such topics as knowledge, belief, evidence, truth, understanding, and explanation. In elaborating these themes in lecture and discussion, an effort was made to relate them to educational notions such as learning, teaching, and curriculum organization, and illustrations were drawn from different teaching areas. Nevertheless, it seemed to me that something more was needed to tie the main thread of the course work to particular regions of teaching with which the students would be individually concerned upon graduation. For this purpose, each student was therefore requested to acquaint himself with the philosophical literature bearing on the foundations of his own teaching subject, and was further asked to write a paper relating such literature to selected aspects of teaching. To facilitate this assignment, students were given bibliographies listing recent philosophical works bearing on the several teaching areas, e.g., books treating of philosophy of mathematics, philosophy of history, philosophy of science, philosophy of language, philosophy of art, etc. It was suggested to students that they might use the assignment as an opportunity to deepen or broaden their grasp of their subjects, and they were encouraged to integrate philosophical with any other materials they deemed relevant, in the writing of their papers.

To my great surprise, I found that the typical student had been simply unaware of the existence of a serious philosophical literature relating to his teaching subject; if, in a rare instance, a student *had* known of such a literature, practically in no case had he himself investigated it. Moreover, although the assignment seemed generally to be undertaken with some trepidation, many students soon reported their delight at finding a new and fundamental source of insight into materials with which they would presently be working as teachers. Repeated trial over the years has led me to judge the assignment a definite success: it has again and again elicited papers worth reading, in which students reasonably well-trained in their teaching subjects were, for the first time, challenged to reflect deeply on the foundations of these subjects, and to relate their reflections to the task of teaching. Both the prior training and the imminent prospect of teaching provided concreteness and focus to the philosophical materials; conversely, these materials were immediately seen to have a significant bearing on the framing of general conceptions and selective principles required in teaching. And the initial purpose of the assignment was, moreover, also fulfilled: the general epistemological themes of the course were themselves heightened and intellectually activated by linkage with the concerns of a particular teaching subject.

I have above referred to general conceptions and selective principles required in teaching, and this is perhaps the central point in seeing the potential contribution of philosophies-of to teacher training. To appreciate the point, we may first examine the particular example of philosophy of science, and notice its complex relations with scientific practice. The time is now long past in which philosophers could pretend to a vantage point of superior certitude to that offered by the sciences themselves. They no longer construe themselves as legislating, from such a vantage point, to the scientific practitioner or as taking sides in scientific controversies, at least in their professional capacity. Their philosophical work, in so far as it is addressed to science, takes its initial departure from scientific practice itself, striving to describe and codify it, and to understand and criticize it from a general epistemological standpoint that is, however, shared by scientists as well. Philosophy of science thus springs from scientific practice, but its descriptive and explanatory effort, like all second-order reflection on practice, has the potentiality of closing the circle, of feeding back into practice and altering it. That it springs from practice does not prevent it from exercising a critical and reformative function; that it exercises such a function does not, on the other hand, mean that it is an indispensable starting point for practice. One can, and regularly does, acquire competence within a field of scientific inquiry without preliminary grounding in philosophy of science. Even the strongest proponents of the value of the latter field of study would not, I believe, wish to argue that every scientist requires prior sophistication in this field in order to do his own job ideally well. It is enough that the field itself exists and is cultivated in such a way that communication with practice is possible.

Contrast this situation with that of the teaching of science. The teacher of science is, of course, also a practitioner, but his practice is of a critically different sort from that of the scientist himself. He needs to have a conception of the field of science as a whole, of its aims, methods, and standards; he needs to have principles for selecting materials and experiences suitable for inducting novices into the field, and he needs to be able to communicate both with novices and with scientific sophisticates. Whereas the particular scientific investigator need have no overall conception of science but requires only sophistication in his special subject matter, the science teacher's subject matter embraces scientific thought itself; his professional purpose, that is to say, can be articulated only in terms of some inclusive conception of scientific activity which it is his object to foster. Whereas the scientific researcher need not at all concern himself with the process of training others for research, the science teacher needs to reflect on the proper selection and organization of scientific materials for educational purposes, and so to presuppose a general perspective on those materials. Whereas, finally, the scientific worker requires only sophistication in the special jargon of his intellectual colleagues, the teacher requires something more—the ability to step out of the inner circle of specialists and to make their jargon intelligible to novices aspiring to sophistication. The teacher requires, in other words, a general conceptual grasp of science and a capacity to formulate and explain its workings to the outsider. But the scope of this requirement is, I suggest, virtually indistinguishable from that of the philosophy of science. No matter what additional resources the teacher may draw on, he needs at least to assume the standpoint of philosophy in performing his work.

Thus it appears the philosophy of science is related to two forms of practice, that of scientific investigation and that of science teaching. But these forms of practice are themselves diverse in level. If philosophy of science is a second-order reflective approach to scientific inquiry, science teaching also incorporates such a second-order reflective approach. The science teacher needs to do other things than reflect on science, to be sure, but whatever he does is likely to be qualified by his second-order reflections on the field of science. Unlike the researcher, he cannot isolate himself within the protective walls of some scientific specialty; he functions willy-nilly as a philosopher in critical aspects of his role. And his training is, correspondingly, likely to profit from the special contributions that philosophy of science offers.

Analogous considerations apply, I believe, to the other teaching subjects as well, for example, to mathematics, to history, to art, to literature, and so forth. This, it seems to me, is the reason why students found the assignment earlier described so pertinent to their work. Their reaction, if it can indeed be generalized, suggests that prevalent conceptions of teacher training are curiously restricted. For these conceptions typically emphasize three features: subject-matter competence, practice teaching, and the psychology and methodology of teaching. Since subject-matter competence is, moreover, interpreted as relating exclusively to the first-order proficiency of the practitioner, no attention is given to the need for a second-order, or philosophical, perspective on the subject matter in question. And since, as I have argued, such a perspective is demanded by the teaching role in any event, the result is that it is gained haphazardly and inefficiently by each teacher, without guidance and without awareness of alternatives. Lacking a systematic and critical introduction of philosophical considerations, dogmatic and incoherent philosophical attitudes are enabled to grow and to proliferate.

It is perhaps worthwhile at this point to attempt a more specific characterization of the contributions that philosophies-of might be expected to make. I have already suggested that the educator, like the philosopher, seeks a general account of those fields represented by teaching subjects, that he requires some reflective grasp of the 'forms of thought' they might be said to embody. To speak of 'forms of thought' is of course a simplification, for what is in question relates not only to inference but also to categorization, perception, evaluation, decision, attitude, and expectation, as crystallized in historical traditions of a variety of sorts. The simplification nevertheless serves to illuminate a critical point, for forms may be embodied as well as articulated. And the successive embodiment of forms of thought, which constitutes their perpetuation, does not itself require an articulate grasp of their general features. To acquire the traditional mental habits of the scientist, that is to say, requires only that one learn how to deal scientifically with some range of problems, and to treat critically of the materials bearing upon them. The philosopher, on the other hand, takes these very mental habits as his object, rather than the scientific problems to which they are, or may be, applied. His task, in short, is to articulate and analyze the forms themselves, and to try to understand their point. He wants to achieve such comprehensive analytical understanding not for some ulterior practical motive, but for its own sake, although he does not, of course, deny that understanding may affect practice.

The educator, by contrast with the philosopher, is concerned with the deliberate processes through which forms of thought may be handed on; he strives not only to understand these processes but to institute or facilitate them, so that the mental habits in question may in fact be properly acquired. Although an articulate grasp of these habits is *not* required for their acquisition, it *is* involved in the task of understanding and facilitating such acquisition. To make his own objectives intelligible, the educator needs to be able to analyze and describe those habits which it is his purpose to hand on to the next generation. An articulate grasp of such habits does not, in general, itself figure

as part of the content he transmits to students; it does not therefore follow that it is of no use to the educator. A parent's
sophisticated understanding of sexuality is of the utmost usefulness in helping him to discuss the issue with his children,
though he would generally be ill advised simply to recount such
understanding to them.

If the philosophy-of a given subject is, thus, directed toward
the analysis and understanding of the form of thought embodied
by the subject, it is of potential use to the educator in clarifying
his own objectives. The educator is not, to be sure, necessarily
concerned with such understanding for its own sake—he needs
it in order to facilitate the acquisition of the mental habits in
question. Certainly, for this larger practical goal, he needs more
than clarity of objectives. Equally, however, no amount of educational experimentation or psychological information can substitute for such clarity.

In so far as the analytical understanding of a form of thought
is the task of the philosophy-of that form, it has, then, a contribution to make to education. But such contribution does not
exhaust its role. Understanding merges with criticism and evaluation, with issues of justification and appraisal. The philosophy
of science, for example, is traditionally concerned not only to
define inductive methods, but to evaluate their epistemological
warrant, not only to describe forms of probabilistic inference,
but to inquire into their justification. Analogously, questions of
aesthetic value, of mathematical certainty, of the reliability of
historical reasoning, of the function of literature, all relate
closely to the question of defining correlated forms and fall
within the philosophies-of those forms.

For the educator, surely, such questions are inescapable. He
cannot define his role simply as it is given by received traditions;
he must be prepared to justify his perpetuation or alteration of
them as a consequence of his efforts. This means that the process
of clarifying his objectives has a critical and normative aspect
to it. He needs, of course, to strive for a clear grasp of the form
of thought embodied in the tradition to which he is heir. But
in taking on the responsibility of educational transmission, he
assumes the obligation of evaluating whatever it is in that tradition he elects to perpetuate. At the risk of oversimplification, we
may say that he requires not only a descriptive but a critical
clarification of the forms of thought represented by his subject.
It goes without saying that philosophies-of do not provide the
educator with firmly established views of justification; on the
contrary, they present him with an array of controversial posi-

tions. But this array, although it does not fix his direction, liberates him from the dogmatisms of ignorance, gives him a realistic apprehension of alternatives, and outlines relevant considerations that have been elaborated in the history of the problem.

The analytical understanding and critical appraisal of the form of thought that the educator takes as his objective provide him with some help in curriculum formation. With a general notion of the form in question, he has some idea of exemplifications in concrete materials to be employed in teaching. To complete his task, he certainly needs to call upon elements outside philosophy; he needs independent acquaintance with materials, and information or hypotheses as to the educational effectiveness of various selections and sequences. But the latter alone are also, in themselves, insufficient. For he is concerned to hand on materials, not just as materials, but as embodiments or exemplifications of form, that is to say, of method, style, aim, approach, and standards. Having a general view of the latter, and an independent knowledge of received materials, he can strive to select, shape, and order exemplifications so as to satisfy the further demands of educational efficiency and comprehensiveness.

In the very process of shaping, philosophies-of make a further contribution, which once more may be illustrated by the philosophy of science. It is clearly a mistake to suppose that the latter field is limited to general accounts of scientific method, or of inductive reasoning, etc. On the contrary, it embraces also the analytical description of historical cases or systematic branches of scientific endeavor in such a way as to bring out their methodological or inferential characteristics. Such analytical description typically proceeds in two phases: first, a refined articulation of the content of the historical inquiry or branch of science in question; and second, a systematic account of the elements of the articulation and their relations, designed primarily to exhibit their methodological or epistemological linkages. Philosophy of science is thus capable of aiding the educator not only in formulating a general conception of scientific method, but also in processing scientific materials so as to display them as embodiments of that method.

Philosophers have traditionally undertaken a further task of significance to education: the tracing of connections between specialized exemplifications of forms of thought and common sense conceptions. They have, that is to say, been concerned to interpret, translate, or explicate the content of such exemplifications in terms that are intelligible to the nonspecialist. To make science generally understandable, they have, for example, tried not only to specify the forms of reasoning implicit in scientific argumentation, but also to translate or reduce particular scientific concepts and theories to those familiar, or at least accessible, to common sense. Although the ways they have construed common sense have varied radically, the function fulfilled by their efforts is nevertheless, I believe, of great significance from an educational point of view. For the educator is constantly in the position not only of representing and advancing specialized exemplifications of thought but also of explaining and interpreting such exemplifications to the outsider, that is, the novice. In this translational or explanatory role, he has in the philosopher an experienced ally.

To summarize, I have outlined four main efforts through which philosophies-of might contribute to education: (1) the analytical description of forms of thought represented by teaching subjects; (2) the evaluation and criticism of such forms of thought; (3) the analysis of specific materials so as to systematize and exhibit them as exemplifications of forms of thought; and (4) the interpretation of particular exemplifications in terms accessible to the novice.

My suggestion has been that philosophies-of constitute a desirable additional input in teacher preparation beyond subject-matter competence, practice in teaching, and educational methodology. If the advantages of such an input are to be fully realized, it is, moreover, desirable that the philosophical dimension be introduced into the training of all those involved in the process of teacher preparation, inclusive of educational administrators, psychologists, methodologists, and curriculum workers. The present suggestion, further, requires more than simply a reorganization of teacher training. On the contrary, if the contributions of philosophies-of for teacher training are to be made practically available, independent scholarly thought needs to be given to the general prospects of relating such philosophies to education, and I believe that this effort may provide an important focus for educational philosophy. A rich body of materials relative to each teaching subject lies ready for such effort, structured in such a way as to make it naturally amenable to educational interests, and inviting to philosophical analysis pointed toward teaching practice.

I am, of course, not advocating that educational philosophy should be *wholly* confined to the direction I have outlined. There is certainly, in my view, a role for more general conceptions, even from the standpoint of a special interest in teacher training. To mention one consideration, the contributions of philosophies-of that are outlined above are altogether internal: they relate, for any given philosophy-of, to the particular teaching area that is its object. But the educator's scope cannot in general be thus confined, even in the case of the teacher whose teaching responsibility is limited to one given subject. For even he must concern himself also with external relations: how, for example, if he is a science teacher, does his subject relate to mathematics or to the arts, or to literature? How is it linked to technology? What are its bearings on human values and the enlightenment of human perception and choice? Analogous questions arise for each teaching subject and they require an attempt to deal with relational issues which outstrip the scope of any particular philosophy-of. Here is the continuing significance of general philosophy—of epistemology, logic, ethics, and aesthetics, for example. If such general considerations are relevant, even in the teaching of a given subject, they bear directly on the explicit question of curriculum integration and constitute therefore a desirable element in the training of curriculum workers as well.

Consider, finally, the fact that teaching subjects cannot be taken without question as exclusive and fixed points of the educational process. The educator needs to consider the possibility of new classifications and interrelations among the subjects not only for educational but also for general intellectual purposes. He must, further, devote his attention to aspects of human development that are too elusive or too central to be encompassed within the framework of subjects; for example, the growth of character and the refinement of the emotions. He ought, moreover, to reflect on schooling as an institution, its organization within society, and its consequences for the career of values. Philosophies-of represent, I believe, a very promising focus for educational philosophy, both with respect to its theoretical development and its potential applications to the training of educators. But this focus should not preclude an insistent and continuing recognition of the significance of general studies, both philosophical and other.

Concepts of education

Part **2**

Is education a discipline?   4

Introduction

Does the *enterprise* of education rest upon a *discipline* of education? Is there some autonomous branch of knowledge underlying educational practice? Does the art of education derive its guiding principles from a distinctive realm of theory?

These questions are most serious when they refer, not to the current state of the sciences, but to the principle of the matter. Granted that we do not now have a discipline of education, is there not necessarily such a discipline to be developed or discovered by investigation? Does not the hope of real educational progress depend, moreover, upon the success with which such investigation is carried forward? This rhetorical way of putting the matter is disarmingly simple and has undeniable persuasiveness. Yet we will do well to examine the grounds on which an affirmative answer might be defended.

Educational practice

The practice of education is surely a discipline, it might be said. Some ways of educating are preferable to others; there must be rules distinguishing the better from the worse practices and enjoining us to choose the better. Educational skill is, furthermore, not instinctive but rather the product of training and experience, leading to a mastery of these rules. Such training and experience, as well as the finished art of the master teacher, serve, finally, to discipline the educator as all art disciplines the artist, through the continual challenge to exercise discretion and judgment, patience and foresight, to sacrifice himself in the quest for excellence, to perfect his understanding and love of his material.[1]

Originally given at a conference on the discipline of education sponsored by the Department of Education, Johns Hopkins University, 1961. Published in the volume that grew out of that conference: John Walton and James L. Kuethe, eds, *The Discipline of Education*, Madison: University of Wisconsin Press, 1963; reprinted by permission of the publisher.

Is education a discipline?

This account of the practice of education is certainly plausible. Yet it does not have the slightest tendency to establish the fact that the practice rests upon some autonomous branch of knowledge distinctive to it. That rules govern educational practice may be sufficient ground for declaring such practice to be a discipline, in one sense of this word. It is no ground for supposing these rules to be drawn from a unique theoretical discipline, in another sense of this word. Engineering is governed by rules, but these rules are not drawn from a special science of engineering.

That educational skill is a result of training and experience may provide another reason for holding the practice of education to be a discipline. It gives no support, however, to the supposition that there must be a distinctive branch of science underlying the practice. Medical skill is a product of training and experience, though it draws upon a host of intellectual disciplines. That medicine is a practical discipline does not imply the existence of a unique science of medicine.

There is, finally, an important analogy between serious teaching and serious art. Each disciplines the agent through challenge. It is, however, fallacious to infer from the fact that an activity possesses disciplinary value, that it must therefore rest upon a distinctive discipline of inquiry. There is no science of poetry, though poetry disciplines and civilizes. Nor does painting, for all its creative challenge, presuppose an autonomous science of painting. We must, in short, be careful to distinguish the ways in which we apply the word discipline to activities in general, from the ways in which we apply it to branches of knowledge in particular, and we must avoid fallacious inferences from the one sort of case to the other.

The educational realm

Let us then resolve to speak here of theoretical disciplines exclusively—of branches of knowledge or bodies of science. Each such discipline, it may be said, strives to offer a complete, systematic account of some realm of things in the world. It seeks a comprehensive body of true principles describing and explaining the realm it takes as its proper object. The realm of physical things is the object of the discipline of physics, whose province thus embraces all significant truths concerning physical objects.

Consider now the realm of things involved in educational processes: schools, subjects, ideas, social practices and traditions, students, teachers, methods, and curricula. Surely this important realm must form the proper object of some single theoretical discipline, comprehending all significant general truths about the processes of education. Unless we are to abandon the assumption that the world is ordered, we must suppose that there is, for each realm, and, in particular, for the educational realm, some special and exclusive discipline, comprising within its scope all those principles capable of describing and explaining the peculiar orders which it exemplifies.

This argument takes the view that there is a one-to-one correlation between realms and disciplines, that not only does each discipline apply to a unique realm, but that each realm supports at least one, and at most one, discipline. If it were not so wrong, this view would be most appealing in its symmetry, embodying, as it does, the time-honored notion that reality and discourse are mirror images of one another.[2]

Unfortunately, however, a variety of disciplines may be supported by elements of the same realm, while some realms seem patently to support no discipline at all. It is not the case that if we were to collect all the significant general truths concerning elements of any given realm, they would fill one and only one box, representing *the* discipline of that realm. Indeed, this notion would appear to harbor a contradiction. For if there were a box for realm A and another for realm B, there would need to be still a third for the realm consisting of A + B, containing truths belonging, on the theory before us, exclusively to the first two boxes.

Much of the appeal of the theory derives from the example of physics, whose domain allegedly comprises *all* truths descriptive and explanatory of the realm of physical objects. But the appeal of this example evaporates once we take a good look at the contents of the physical realm. Some physical objects are, after all, linguistic tokens, some are fossils, some are plants or animals, some are people. Even the hardiest physicalist will find it embarrassing to maintain that the truths comprising linguistics, paleontology, biology, anthropology, and psychology belong, even in principle, to the single discipline of physics. And while chemistry is perhaps in principle easier to think of as reducible to physics, it is not (as construed now and in prior years) *actually* thus reducible though it applies to the same realm. It becomes obvious upon reflection that disciplines quite distinct in content and manner of expression may be supported by the same realm of things.[3] At its best, physicalism is thus a doctrine concerning the elements to which disciplines apply, rather than a doctrine claiming exhaustiveness for the discipline of physics.

Is education a discipline?

If the realm of physical objects is taken as our model for the educational realm, we have no reason to suppose that there is at most one theoretical discipline of education, comprising all those general descriptive and explanatory truths concerning the elements of education. Nor, considering certain other realms as examples, do we have any reason to suppose that every realm must support at least one discipline, on pain of violating some general assumption of an ordered universe. There is no discipline associated with the realm of chairs, but this does not mean that the mechanical behavior of chairs presents a baffling mystery to our sense of order. Chairs, as well as all other classes of physical objects, fall under the general principles of physics. It is clearly fallacious to infer, from the fact that every discipline takes some realm of things as its object, that therefore every realm of things must be the object of some discipline. If there is, in fact, no special discipline of education, it does not in the least follow that the realm of education must remain opaque to our understanding.

Educational phenomena

We have criticized the notion of a one-to-one correlation between theoretical disciplines and realms of things. Disciplines may differ, we have said, despite the fact that they are associated with the same range of objects. Perhaps the reason is that they give accounts of different classes of phenomena manifested by these selfsame objects or, alternatively, of different classes of aspects or properties possessed by them.

The idea is a natural one. Consider John Smith. His weight is a physical datum, his pulse a biological datum, and his conversation a psychological datum. He is simultaneously subject to physical, biological, and psychological analysis. What is more plausible than to suppose that, in addition to the concrete John Smith before us, there are a variety of related Platonic entities to be reckoned with, namely, the physical, the biological, and the psychological phenomena manifested by him? Each such set of phenomena, it might be said, forms the basis of some discipline applicable to Smith, providing an ethereal bridge between Smith the object and the truths by which he is described within this particular discipline.

The variety of disciplines, on this view, thus arises out of the variety of types of phenomena. To each such type corresponds a single discipline, and every discipline corresponds to some single type. The existence of educational phenomena thus guarantees, at least in principle, a unique discipline of education, though, admittedly, any range of objects manifesting educational phenomena will certainly be manifesting other sorts of phenomena as well, and so be analyzable by several disciplines at once.

There is a certain attractiveness to this view, and it accords well with much of our ordinary thinking and talking; but it will not withstand serious analysis. Objections analogous to those previously discussed present themselves immediately. Not every set of aspects, properties, or phenomena supports a separate discipline. If there is no science of the class of chairs, neither is there a science of the phenomenon of chairhood. Nor is it the case that at most one discipline formulates the truth concerning any given set of phenomena. It is, to be sure, undeniable that linguistic studies, for example, do not address themselves to the physical properties of their subject matter, but such properties surely enter into disciplines other than physics, for example, chemistry and biology.

Formally, too, the contradiction noted above lurks here as well. If the class of phenomena K and the class of phenomena L have unique disciplines associated with them, and there is also a unique discipline for the class K + L, either some truths fall into two boxes or some box is not completely filled. At this point, however, the possibility of a new philosophical move presents itself. We may declare that we have an independent criterion for determining 'pure' classes of phenomena and that this criterion prevents the formation of K + L, upon which the troublesome contradiction depends. Putting the matter another way, the one-to-one correlation of disciplines and phenomenal classes is now proposed to hold only for pure phenomenal classes, as determined by our supposed independent criterion. This criterion rules out, for example, the class of physical-biological phenomena, recognizing only the two classes of purely physical and purely biological phenomena. This move was inappropriate before, with respect to objects, for the notion of a purely biological or purely physical object is inconceivable. The notion of a purely biological or physical aspect, property, or phenomenon, however, is not at all inconceivable.

The Platonizing of our problem thus does accomplish something new by comparison with the previous formulation. In particular, it avoids the inconsistency noted, and it allows several disciplines to apply to the same realm of objects, claiming only a one-to-one correlation with pure classes of phenomena associated with this realm. But it fails to remove the other objections noted.

For it will still be difficult to maintain that every pure class of phenomena supports a discipline. And it will still be true that more than one discipline is related to a given pure class of phenomena as, for example, anthropology and sociology are both concerned with social phenomena. Further, it is no longer clear that we still have an argument for the existence of an educational discipline, since it is not clear that educational phenomena are pure.

It might be said that at least one of the above criticisms is unfair: social phenomena are not pure; they must be split into anthropological and sociological phenomena, each group supporting at most one discipline. But how do we know this? What, after all, *is* our criterion for determining pure classes of phenomena? What, indeed, is a phenomenon, aspect, or property, as distinct from the thing that manifests it and the word that attributes it?[4] Presumably, the mass of a particular painting by Monet is one of its physical phenomena or aspects, while its being an instance of French impressionism is not. Presumably, Khrushchev's power is a sociological property, unlike his height, volume, and chemical composition, which are not. Are not these decisions, however, perfectly parallel to the judgments by which we decide that the term 'mass' is a physical term while the term 'instance of French impressionism' is not, that the term 'power' belongs to the vocabulary of sociology, whereas the terms employed in formulating height, volume, and chemical descriptions do not? This question gives rise to the nagging suspicion that the language of phenomena is a parasite on the language of language, that phenomena have no independent life but are projected on the world by the terms we use, that they are mere shadows cast on objects by our descriptions of them. Why not clarify the situation by eliminating this shadow world completely, and focusing our attention directly on the language in which our accepted descriptions and explanations of things are expressed?

Educational terms

We began by trying to construe theoretical disciplines in terms of peculiar realms of objects and found this course unsatisfactory. The alternative attempt to attach such disciplines to distinctive classes of pure phenomena turned out to be equally frustrating, for new as well as old reasons. Shall we fare better by turning from objects and phenomena to words?

Some clear pitfalls in this new course are immediately evident.

We must not, for example, proceed to explain the disciplines as characterized by special vocabularies, and then blithely go on to delimit these vocabularies in terms of what is required to account for distinct realms of phenomena or objects. For this would raise the old difficulties again. Nor must we characterize the discipline of physics, for instance, as one formulated in physical terms—understanding by *physical term* a term that is used in formulating physics. For such a procedure would be clearly circular. What then *can* be done?

The attractiveness of the present idea lies in the fact that the several theoretical disciplines may be construed as several bodies of systematized information, each such body presumably expressed by a distinctive linguistic apparatus. Assume, for simplicity's sake, a common core of logical terms and a common syntax for all disciplines. The extralogical vocabulary of each will then differ from that of each other in at least some degree. Thus, for example, biology, but not physics, will contain the extralogical term 'cell,' though both share a common logical structure. Some degree of overlap in vocabularies is thus compatible with the distinctiveness of each, taken as a whole. Can we not then specify the domain of each discipline as what is expressible by means of the extralogical vocabulary associated with it, with the help of logic and in accord with the assumed standard syntax? And is not a discipline of education thus guaranteed by the fact that the vocabulary of education is, at least in part, distinctive?

There are complex refinements to be made before the present idea can be put with even minimal clarity. Consider, for example, the extralogical vocabulary of biology; let us designate this vocabulary as B. Now let us designate the extralogical vocabulary of chemistry as C. We may reasonably assume that B overlaps C, that is, that certain extralogical terms belong to both the biological and the chemical vocabularies. How shall we now classify a statement S, whose extralogical constituents are all drawn from the area of overlap? Shall we, in particular, assign S to the discipline of biology or to the discipline of chemistry?

We may attempt to settle this question by introducing some notion of presuppositional order among the disciplines. We assume, for example, that physics presupposes logic, that chemistry presupposes physics and is in turn presupposed by biology. Now if S is composed of extralogical terms wholly drawn from the overlap of the biological and chemical vocabularies, but not at all from the overlap of both of these with physics, then we assign S to chemistry, since biology presupposes chemistry. In Morton White's phrase, S contains no *specifically* biological terms, but only specifically chemical terms, except for logic.[5]

What shall we now do with a statement of another sort, T, which *does* contain some specifically biological terms, as well as some specifically chemical terms, but no other extralogical terms? Here we may follow the rule recently suggested by White, that a statement is to be classified under a given discipline if, besides containing terms specific to that discipline, all other contained terms are specific to disciplines presupposed by it.[6] Thus T is to be assigned to biology.

Let us here waive the difficult question as to how the order of presupposition is to be interpreted, as well as all other problems arising out of the foregoing refinements. The basic idea is now that the province of a discipline is to be construed in terms of its specific extralogical vocabulary as well as its standing in the order of presupposition. Does it not now follow, from the existence of a specific educational vocabulary, that there must be a discipline of education?

Before we say 'yes' to the last question, we must look critically at the basic idea underlying it. As a matter of fact, the general proposal has untenable consequences. Suppose, for example, that the terms 'table' and 'round' are each definable in physical terminology. Then the true statement, 'Some tables are not round,' is expressible in the specific language of physics. Yet this statement surely does not belong to the discipline of physics. Indeed, if this statement were considered to belong to physics because translatable into physical terms, its negation, 'All tables are round,' would also belong to physics by the same token, and the discipline of physics would turn out self-contradictory. Neither statement, in fact, belongs to the body of physical theories and laws, nor does either one follow from these. The term 'table,' though definable in physical terms, is, moreover, not a term that can properly be said to belong to the discipline of physics. It does not now figure in the formulation of physical laws or theories, nor is it ever likely to do so. The range of a discipline, if these reflections are correct, is considerably narrower than what is theoretically expressible by means of the discipline's distinctive linguistic apparatus. Much of what is thus expressible falls outside the discipline, and two disciplines may conceivably share the same apparatus. The range of a discipline thus seems to be a function, not of the expressive power of a given linguistic apparatus, but rather of the availability of a body of laws and theories which have been formulated and established within its scope. The point may be put in terms of the reduction of one discipline to another. If one discipline is to be reduced to a second, it will not in general be enough to show its terminology to be wholly definable by means of the second discipline's terminology. It will, in addition, be necessary to show its principles to be derivable from those of the second discipline.[7] This is another way of saying that the range of a discipline is set by a body of laws and theories, rather than by a particular vocabulary of terms.

While the derivation of a given statement from the principles of a particular discipline shows that the statement has indeed been reduced to, and hence belongs to, that discipline, it does *not* follow that every unreduced statement belongs to *some other* discipline. Recall our recent statement, 'Some tables are not round.' Though we may here assume each of its extralogical terms to be definable by means of the vocabulary of physics, it does not, I have argued, belong to the discipline of physics. Nor is there any necessity of supposing that, because it falls outside physics, it must therefore fall within the scope of some other discipline.

Note that, in the statement we have just considered, every extralogical term is definable in physical terminology and yet the statement as a whole is not 'significant' in any theoretical sense; it is not likely to figure as a principle of any scientific discipline, though it is true. In general, the fact that a term is definable within the language of a discipline in no way guarantees that there must be significant principles formulable with its help. Carl Hempel some years ago illustrated an argument of his by inventing the term 'hage.'[8] A person's hage is his height, in inches, multiplied by his age, in years. Now my hage happens to be 2,698. Assume that I can be identified by my present spatio-temporal position, within the language of physics. It is obvious that, though the object with this position can then be said, within physical terminology, to have a hage of 2,698, this statement is not part of the discipline of physics. There is, furthermore, surely no necessity that the term 'hage' will be fruitful in the formulation of any theoretical or lawlike principle within any discipline, despite the fact that it is definable in physical terms by means of which significant principles are expressed.[9]

Is it not even more obvious that disciplines cannot be created simply by producing new terms not definable within the vocabularies of established disciplines? Assume that educational terminology is distinctive, and thus allows us to express more than could be expressed without it. The crucial question remains whether this surplus is scientifically significant: Are there laws and theories forming a systematic and comprehensive body of assertions that are both expressible by means of this terminology and true, or at least, interesting in the scientific sense, and well supported? This condition is not necessarily met by every term. The fact that a term belongs to none of the hitherto established disciplines does not therefore guarantee that there must be some as-yet-undiscovered discipline to which it will belong. Whether the condition will in fact be met in a given case is determinable, if at all, by investigation rather than by *a priori* arguments. The mere distinctiveness of educational terminology, were it established, would not in itself guarantee the existence of a discipline of education.

Educational principles

I have suggested that disciplines are dependent on the availability of established scientific principles, that is, theories and laws, and that the terms of a discipline are those by means of which such principles are formulated. Does this imply that there is no connection between a given discipline and terms or statements that fall outside it? I think the answer is 'no.' For to suppose that there is no connection is to construe the disciplines as completely isolated and self-contained. It is to deny the applicability of the disciplines to the concrete affairs of everyday life.

To illustrate: imagine that someone drops a lighted cigar on my new coffee table and burns it. The question, 'Why did my new coffee table show a burn when I came back into the parlor with the cheese?' is a question to which science supplies a relevant answer. Suitably supplemented with the particulars of the case, relevant principles explain the disaster, despite the fact that science includes no laws of the burning of new coffee tables nor references to cheese or parlors. The term 'abstract painting' is not, I should think, definable (at least in any obvious way) in physical terms, but physics will explain why a particular abstract painting fell from the wall yesterday. The terms peculiar to common affairs may belong to no discipline at all, but they normally figure in applying the disciplines to life. This they do in helping to formulate both the initial problems arising in practice and those particulars that serve to bring problematic cases within the scope of disciplinary principles.

Suppose, now, that the terms peculiar to educational institutions and practices never yield a discipline of education in the sense outlined. Does this imply that education is cut off from all established disciplines, and must forever lack theoretical illumination? If the previous considerations are correct, the answer must clearly be in the negative. The problems of education, the questions arising in educational practice, will be framed in familiar educational terms. Whatever explanatory principles are at all relevant will receive their educational applications through being linked with these terms. The latter may not figure explicitly within the principles themselves, but to suppose these principles therefore irrelevant is to suppose an absurdity. It is to suppose, in effect, that these principles are generally useless because generally inapplicable.

A crucial issue, it thus seems to me, is whether we can establish reliable principles to explain how and why children learn, schools develop, curricula change, ideals conflict, perceptions alter, societies differ, standards of taste and culture are formed. That *any* discipline is likely to be developed capable of answering these questions systematically and reliably is still a matter of some controversy. Ernest Nagel, a distinguished student of logical and methodological issues in the social sciences, has recently written: [10]

> In no area of social inquiry has a body of general laws been established, comparable with outstanding theories in the natural sciences in scope of explanatory power or in capacity to yield precise and reliable predictions... Many social scientists are of the opinion, moreover, that the time is not yet ripe even for theories designed to explain systematically only quite limited ranges of social phenomena... To a considerable extent, the problems investigated in many current centers of empirical social research are admittedly problems of moderate and often unimpressive dimensions... In short, the social sciences today possess no wide ranging systems of explanations judged as adequate by a majority of professionally competent students, and they are characterized by serious disagreements on methodological as well as substantive questions.

The problem, it seems to me, is thus to advance the state of social inquiry—in particular, of all those studies that seem likely to yield explanatory principles relevant to the concerns of education.[11] Whether, however, it turns out that one or several theoretical disciplines develop, and whether any of these is a discipline of education specifically, seem to me quite unimportant issues.

As educators, we shall continue to ask all sorts of questions arising in the course of our work. If the arguments presented above are at all convincing, we ought not to isolate ourselves from attempts to formulate principles relevant to our work, no matter what their disciplinary labels. Nor ought we to build our professional identity upon the faith that a unique discipline of education will one day be found. Rather, we should encourage relevant investigations by psychologists, anthropologists, sociologists, economists, educationalists, and still others, and we should strive to link them with the concerns of schooling. There is surely enough substance in such an enterprise to support a genuine and important professional identity, indeed, several such identities. If it turns out that, in the place of a unique discipline of education, we get a variety of systematized laws and principles, *applicable* to the practice of education, I cannot see that we will have serious cause for complaint.

Notes

1 See, in this connection, M. Black, 'Education as Art and Discipline, *Ethics*, LIV (1944), 290-4; reprinted in I. Scheffler, ed., *Philosophy and Education*, Boston: Allyn & Bacon, 1958.

2 For a general discussion, see Nelson Goodman, 'The Way the World Is,' *Review of Metaphysics*, XIV (1960), 48-56.

3 The independence of ontology from the conceptual apparatus of a theory is discussed in W. V. Quine, *From a Logical Point of View*, Cambridge: Harvard University Press, 1953, particularly Chap. 7. A criticism of the notion that we explain *objects* is contained in the last section of my 'Explanation, Prediction, and Abstraction,' *British Journal for the Philosophy of Science*, VII (1957), 293-309.

4 See, in this connection, Nelson Goodman, 'On Likeness of Meaning,' *Analysis*, X (1949), 1-7, reprinted in L. Linsky, ed., *Semantics and the Philosophy of Language*, Urbana: University of Illinois Press, 1952; and M. White, *Toward Reunion in Philosophy*, Cambridge: Harvard University Press, 1956.

5 See M. White, 'Historical Explanation,' *Mind*, LII (1943), reprinted with Postscript, in P. Gardiner, *Theories of History*, Chicago: Free Press, 1959, where the attempt is made to determine the status of history as an independent discipline.

6 See his reply to a query by the present writer, in P. Gardiner, *Theories of History*, p. 372.

7 See E. Nagel, 'The Meaning of Reduction in the Natural Sciences,' in R. C. Stauffer, ed., *Science and Civilization*, Madison: University of Wisconsin Press, 1949, and also Nagel, *The Structure of Science*, New York: Harcourt, Brace & World, 1961.

8 C. G. Hempel, *Fundamentals of Concept Formation in Empirical Science*, Chicago: University of Chicago Press, 1952, p. 46. I have here taken the liberty of specifying inches rather than Hempel's millimeters.

9 By 'principles' I here intend lawlike principles rather than bare

generalizations. See Nelson Goodman, *Fact, Fiction, and Forecast,*
2nd ed., Indianapolis: Bobbs-Merrill, 1965.

10 E. Nagel, *The Structure of Science,* pp. 447-9.

11 See the related comments in my *The Language of Education,*
Springfield, Ill.: Thomas, 1960, Chap. 4, pp. 71-5.

5 Concepts of education: Reflections on the current scene

The dominant ideological trend in American education today is, it seems to me, a continuing rejection of the ideas and values associated with progressivism. If the main thrust of progressive ideas represented, in Morton White's[1] phrase, a revolt against formalism, we are currently witnessing the high tide of a counter-revolutionary return to formalism.

The counter-revolution proceeds along many fronts. Most obvious, perhaps, is the widespread and forceful emphasis on academic values in the economy of educational ideals. The prevalent slogans have all shifted out of the motivational and into the cognitive mode: we now hear constantly of 'excellence,' 'mastery,' 'structure,' and 'discipline' where we once heard of 'adjustment,' 'interest,' 'growth,' and 'self-expression.' In place of the autonomous humanistic ideal of self-development, and the progressive concern with the child as the center of the educational process, we now find an increasing appeal to the model of the academic disciplines, and an increasing effort to shape schooling in their image.

The new primacy of the academic is not, however, a development in a vacuum. It is clearly related to the urgency of national needs in the present period of international crisis and technological transformation. It is no accident, therefore, that the present return to formalism is not equally concerned with all the academic disciplines; unlike the old formalism rooted in classical studies, it pushes hardest for the scientific, mathematical, and technical studies within the academic complex.

Presented to the 1963 Summer Institute for Administrators of Pupil Personnel Services at the Harvard Graduate School of Education. Published in Edward Landy and Paul A. Perry, eds, *Guidance in American Education: Backgrounds and Prospects*, Cambridge: Harvard Graduate School of Education (distributed by Harvard University Press), 1964; reprinted by permission of the publishers. The paper is a response to the academic and disciplinary emphases of the period and should be compared with essay 10, written in response to later, and contrasting, emphases on educational relevance. (Extracts here and following from Ryle, *The Concept of Mind*, Hutchinson and Harper & Row, 1949, by permission of the author and publishers.)

Nor is this return to formalism manifested only by a stress on academic values and 'hard education.' It appears also in the vast current emphasis on educational technology, the development of devices, programs and new curricula for the more efficient packaging and distribution of knowledge. What was, in the days of progressivism, a broad concern for scientific inquiry into processes of growth, perception, and socialization has, in the name of hardheaded research and development, become more and more a preoccupation with the hard facts comprising educational content, and their optimal ordering for transmission to the student. We have here, it seems to me, a new discovery of the old transmission model of education, and a concomitant drive to increase the efficiency with which facts are transmitted from the disciplines into the student's mind.

I have described the formalist counter-revolution in a somewhat negative tone, but I do not wholly deplore it. There are, it seems to me, some good reasons that might be given in justification of the current trend. The contemporary world presents us with a variety of serious problems that amount to a challenge, a challenge we can properly meet only if we retain our scientific and technological momentum. This momentum itself creates vast problems as it transforms our ways of working, thinking, and living together in community. The upshot is a clearly reasonable demand for greater educational attention to science, mathematics, and technology.

Furthermore, any improvement in the efficiency with which factual knowledge can be processed and disseminated is, I should think, clearly a good, taken in itself. There is no positive virtue in inefficient teaching of factual materials. Advances in educational technology that enable the raising of academic standards and the speedier diffusion of new knowledge in the school are, other things being equal, outcomes to be desired and welcomed.

Finally, it must be admitted that progressivism did have its shortcomings. It tended to underplay the systematic and objective corpus of knowledge and to tie it too closely to practical social concerns. As Morris R. Cohen[2] once remarked of Dewey's work, it stressed the value rather than the dignity of thought. It exaggerated the relevance of scientific modes of thought for all areas of experience. In practice, it brought the personal and motivational aspects of education to the fore, and placed too much responsibility for these on teacher and school.

The current formalist counter-revolution thus seems to me to have some strong considerations in its favor. Like all revolutions, however, it may, if unchecked, run to perilous excesses. My wish is not that it should be destroyed, but only contained.

Clearly, there are, to begin with, obvious limitations to the arguments brought forward in its favor. If our survival as a democracy requires greater emphasis on science and technology, it also requires increased historical and political sophistication and a greater understanding of the ideas and forces that move the minds of men. If the growth of science and technology creates radical human problems, surely we need not only technical sophistication but also deeper knowledge of human affairs in order to cope with them. If improvements in educational efficiency are to be welcomed, other things being equal, can we assume that other things are, in fact, equal? If progressivism under-emphasized the academic and the disciplinary aspects of education, does this mean that its individual and humanistic focus has no longer any relevance at all for education?

Such considerations suggest that the formalist counter-revolution must be watched with a critical eye, and contained within reasonable bounds. If it is unchecked and allowed to run its course it will, I fear, seriously endanger the processes of schooling by a severe narrowing of our educational perspective.

Such a narrowing of perspective may be pictured at many levels; I shall briefly paint the dangers as they relate to the scope of education, the role of the teacher, and the concept of educational method. First, it seems to me that the proper scope of education is as large as civilization itself. The basic task of education, in my view, is to humanize and civilize, to introduce each generation afresh to all the great modes of human experience: to science and art, history and poetry, morality and religion, languages and philosophy. In this way, education serves both to pass on the varied habits of mind that make up civilized culture and, at the same time, to form the child into an autonomous participant in such culture. If we narrow the scope of education, we narrow our operative conception of civilization, and we impoverish the meaning of participation in civilized community. C. P. Snow[3] has urged the importance of literary as well as scientific culture, and Sidney Hook[4] has recently urged the importance of a third culture, represented by history, politics and social science. But can we properly omit art, morality, classics and philosophy? To raise the question is to begin to realize what it means to say that education is coincident with the scope of civilization itself. A limitation to the cognitive and the academic, not to say the hard core of science, mathematics and technology, would, in my view, be a disaster.

Consider now the impact of a runaway formalism on the role

of the teacher. The transmission model of education, coupled with the drive for increased efficiency, tends to foster the view of the teacher as a minor technician within an industrial process. The over-all goals are set in advance in terms of national needs, the curricular materials prepackaged by the disciplinary experts, the methods developed by educational engineers—and the teacher's job is just to supervise the last operational stage, the methodical insertion of ordered facts into the student's mind. Teacher competence is to be judged (at most) in terms of academic mastery and pedagogical dexterity, and teacher education becomes identified with training in the subject, coupled with training in the approved methods of teaching.

In my view, this picture is radically wrong. The teacher in a free society is not just a technician. He ought to have a voice in shaping the purposes of the whole educational enterprise. In any event, he influences students not just by what he *does* but by what he *is*, not just by the *facts* he provides but by the *questions* he provokes. He needs a basic flexibility of mind, a capacity to step outside his subject and consider it from without together with his student, a fundamental respect for his student's mind, and a willingness to encourage new ideas, doubts, questions, and puzzlements. If he is to fulfill his function properly, he must be viewed not just as a technician but as a free mind alive to radical questions concerning the foundations of his subject, its relations to other areas, and its applications in society. He must be trained not just as an applied specialist but as a free and critical intellect.

Imagine, finally, the narrowing effect on educational method involved in overreliance on the transmission model. Facts are, after all, not simple things such as trees, rocks, or chairs. They are clothed in concepts with theoretical ramifications, and they need to be formulated, selected, and rendered intelligible, as well as simply transmitted. Further, the student needs to learn how to use them intelligently; it is possible to possess the facts but to let them rot or apply them stupidly. 'Stupidity,' as Gilbert Ryle has put it, 'is not the same thing, or the same sort of thing, as ignorance. There is no incompatibility between being well-informed and being silly, and a person who has a good nose for arguments or jokes may have a bad head for facts.'[5]

Nor should the appeal to slogans referring to the *intellect* mislead us. For to construe the intellect in terms of possession of facts or academic mastery rather than schooled intelligence is itself a distortion, as Ryle has brilliantly argued in *The Concept of Mind*.[6] It seems to me, moreover, that the concept of *ration-*

ality is even broader than that of intelligence, involving simply the capacity to grasp principles and purposes, and to evaluate them critically in the light of reasons that might be put forward in public discussion. Rationality is thus, as I view it, the ability to participate in critical and open evaluation of rules and principles in any area of life. To initiate the child into the rational life is to engage him in the critical dialogues that relate to every area of civilization: to science and art, morality and philosophy, history and government. It is to nourish his curiosity and critical judgment as well as his responsibility for choices of belief and conduct. Such a conception goes far beyond the notion of academic mastery of factual subject matter, and far beyond the transmission model.

I should like, now, in fact, to propose that the ideal of rationality offers us a way of containing the current formalist trend, while preserving what is best in the humanistic and progressive tradition. This ideal is not subject to criticisms validly directed against progressivism; it does not exalt the practical as against the theoretical, the scientific as against the nonscientific, the value as against the dignity of thought. Nor does it entail a special centrality for personal and motivational aspects of education. On the other hand, it does involve a primary concern for the free and critical judgment of the free mind in all realms, and a pervasive attempt to strengthen its autonomy and responsibility.

'Rationality,' I am well aware, has an old-fashioned ring to it in many quarters, and I do not expect my proposal to be readily appealing. But I am, after all, not suggesting that it belongs to a special faculty of the mind called *Reason*, nor am I identifying it with some restricted set of rules for making logical deductions. Rationality, as I see it, is a matter of *reasons*, and to take it as a fundamental educational ideal is to make as pervasive as possible the free and critical quest for reasons, in all realms of study.

This notion, as I argued in *The Language of Education*,[7] is peculiar to the ordinary concept of teaching, as differentiated from mere acquisition of beliefs, for beliefs can be acquired or transferred through mere unthinking contact, propaganda, indoctrination, or brainwashing. Teaching, by contrast, engages the mind, no matter what the subject matter. The teacher is prepared to *explain*, that is, to acknowledge the student's right to ask for reasons and his concomitant right to exercise his judgment on the merits of the case. Teaching is, in this standard sense, an initiation into open rational discussion.

In recent polemics against progressivism, the attacks have been almost wholly directed against John Dewey. Certainly, there are many distinctive ideas and formulations for which Dewey is responsible, but in the matter of emphasizing the free judgment of the child as against fixed adult curricula imposed from above, Dewey is simply the spokesman of a fundamental philosophical tradition of the West. Socrates, the greatest teacher in this tradition, had, after all, no curriculum, no facts, no answers, no formulae. He had only questions, and the willingness to follow the argument wherever it might lead. He was totally uninterested in the social class, erudition, or IQ of his friends and students— interested only in engaging them in a critical quest for truth.

St Augustine, in his brilliant dialogue, *De Magistro*,[8] criticized the theory that knowledge could be transmitted through language; his argument is well worth the attention of educators today. In Augustine's view, the teacher's task is to prompt the student to confront reality for himself so that his mind may be illuminated by the truth.

In the work of the great eighteenth-century philosopher, Immanuel Kant,[9] we find a clear conception of rationality as the basis not only of the intellectual but of the moral life. Rationality, for Kant, means impartiality and fairness of judgment; the conforming of one's actions to general rules which one has freely accepted for oneself. If, for example, I act not expediently but on principle, and submit myself equally to those rules which govern all, I treat others as ends, not merely as means to be used; this is rationality in the realm of conduct.

It is no accident that Kant connects rationality not only with science but with moral conduct, and indeed with the concept of a democracy, in his notion of a 'kingdom of ends.' For the notion of being rational is not simply, or even primarily, a theoretical or cognitive idea; it applies to social conduct as well. In Kant's view, it underlies the concepts of justice and the rule of law. If I am rational, I am willing to respect others, and to treat their arguments and claims on an equal basis with my own, to be decided on their merits. I thus acknowledge that I may be wrong and that others may be right. The democratic ideal is just to institutionalize such rationality in matters of public concern, to support the critical and open review of social principles by all capable members of the community.

I have been arguing that the ideal of rationality is capable of providing a unifying and liberal focus for education, of tempering the extremes of formalism and preserving what is most precious in the humanistic and progressive tradition. I should like to comment upon one special problem that is particularly urgent and pressing today: the problem of moral education in the schools. This is a problem that is (in my opinion) clearly beyond the competence of formalism to deal with. If we confine education to the intellect and interpret the intellect in academic terms, is it, after all, surprising that moral and spiritual values become an utter mystery? Is it any wonder that the solution seems to lie in some external or artificial device such as a school prayer or period of meditation?

The constructive challenge to the educator, resulting from the recent Supreme Court decision on school prayers, as Professor Paul Freund has wisely remarked, is to build moral and character education integrally into the school's work by emphasizing the process of rational discussion in relation to human affairs and moral issues. This suggestion is clearly congenial to the proposal I have been advocating here. The relevance of rationality to character seems to me very great indeed. To learn to be critical while respecting one's colleagues in discussion, to learn to recognize one's fallibility, to commit oneself to following the argument on its merits and to take the consequences, to be sensitive to the standpoint of other persons with conflicting claims and different centers of experience, to learn to judge fairly and to take the responsibility for one's own judgments—these are lessons of morality and character no less than cognitive virtues. They are lessons that are relevant to all phases of education, and they cannot be taught by machine, for they grow out of rational intercourse with other persons. The teacher as agent in this process is not primarily an expert authority on some realm of fact, nor a technician in an industrial enterprise. He is a *person* who can, in the exercise of his special authority, show his respect for his students' minds, his willingness to entertain their serious questions, and his commitment to high standards of impartial and critical judgment.

We are indeed faced by important challenges from within and without, and we cannot, without peril, ignore either the external or the internal dangers. But if we give up a broad and liberal perspective on education while attempting to meet these challenges, we risk a fatal impoverishment of our culture and a deadening of intellectual and moral initiative. Whatever we do, I believe we ought to keep uppermost the ideal of rationality and its emphasis on the critical, questioning, responsible, free mind.

In 1832, John Stuart Mill published an essay *On Genius*[10] in which he criticized the education of his day and compared it adversely to the education of the ancients. His essay (though containing elements of faculty psychology) is one of the most powerful and relevant criticisms of pure formalism that I know. He praises Greek education thus:

> Education *then* consisted not in giving what is called knowledge, that is, grinding down other men's ideas to a convenient size, and administering them in the form of *cram* —it was a series of exercises to form the thinking faculty itself, that the mind, being active and vigorous, might go forth and know. The studies of the closet were combined with, and were intended as, a preparation for the pursuits of active life. This was the education to form great statesmen, great orators, great warriors, great poets, great architects, great sculptors, great philosophers; because, once for all, it formed *men*, and not mere knowledge-boxes; and the men being men, had minds, and could apply them to the work, whatever it might be, which circumstances had given them to perform.

By contrast, he complains, 'modern education is all *cram*... The world already knows everything, and has only to tell it to its children.' 'Is it any wonder,' he asks, 'that the ten centuries of England or France cannot produce as many illustrious names as the hundred and fifty years of little Greece?'

The remedy? Mill sees it in

> the distinct recognition that the end of education is not to *teach*, but to fit the mind for learning from its own consciousness and observation; that we have occasion for this power under ever-varying circumstances, for which no routine or rule of thumb can possibly make provision. Let all *cram* be ruthlessly discarded. Let each person be made to feel that in other things he may believe upon trust—if he finds a trustworthy authority —but that in the line of his peculiar duty, and in the line of the duties common to all men, it is his business to *know*. Let the feelings of society cease to stigmatize independent thinking, and divide its censure between a lazy dereliction of the duty and privilege of thought, and the overweening self-conceit of a half-thinker, who rushes to his conclusions without taking the trouble to understand the thoughts of other men. Were all this done, there would be no complaint of any want of genius in modern times. But when will that hour come? Though it come not at all, yet is it not less your duty and mine to strive for it,—and first to do what is certainly and absolutely in our power, to realize it in our own persons.

Notes

1 Morton White, *Social Thought in America, The Revolt Against Formalism*, Boston: Beacon Press, 1957 (first published 1949).
2 Morris Raphael Cohen, *A Preface to Logic*, New York: Meridian Books, 1956, p. 209. The remark first appeared in Cohen's review of Dewey's *Essays in Experimental Logic*, in *The New Republic*, 1916, Vol. 8, p. 118. Cohen wrote about Dewey, 'He is one of the very few to insist on the high value of thought. But note, it is the value, not the dignity, of thought that he emphasizes.'
3 C. P. Snow, *The Two Cultures and the Scientific Revolution*, New York: Cambridge University Press, 1959.
4 Sidney Hook, *Education for Modern Man*, new ed., New York: Knopf, 1963, pp. 22 ff.
5 Gilbert Ryle, *The Concept of Mind*, London: Hutchinson, 1949, p. 25.
6 *Ibid.*, Chap. 9.
7 Israel Scheffler, *The Language of Education*, Springfield, Ill.: Thomas, 1960, pp. 57-9. See also Richard Peters, *Authority, Responsibility and Education*, London: Allen & Unwin, 1959, especially Chap. 7.
8 A recent book, which presents critical selections from this dialogue, together with an interpretive essay on Augustine in the context of educational thought, is Kingsley Price, *Education and Philosophical Thought*, Boston: Allyn & Bacon, 1962.
9 See, for example, the selections in 'Theory of Ethics' in Theodore Meyer Greene, ed., *Kant Selections*, New York: Scribner, 1929; and the chapter on Kant in Kingsley Price, *op. cit.*
10 See Kingsley Price, *op. cit.*, Chap. ix, for critical selections from this essay and interpretive discussion.

Philosophical models of teaching

6

Introduction

Teaching may be characterized as an activity aimed at the achievement of learning, and practiced in such manner as to respect the student's intellectual integrity and capacity for independent judgment. Such a characterization is important for at least two reasons: first, it brings out the intentional nature of teaching, the fact that teaching is a distinctive goal-oriented activity, rather than a distinctively patterned sequence ot behavioral steps executed by the teacher. Second, it differentiates the activity of teaching from such other activities as propaganda, conditioning, suggestion, and indoctrination, which are aimed at modifying the person but strive at all costs to avoid a genuine engagement of his judgment on underlying issues.

This characterization of teaching, which I believe to be correct, fails, nevertheless, to answer certain critical questions of the teacher: What sort of learning shall I aim to achieve? In what does such learning consist? How shall I strive to achieve it? Such questions are, respectively, normative, epistemological, and empirical in import, and the answers that are provided for them give point and substance to the educational enterprise. Rather than try to separate these questions, however, and deal with each abstractly and explicitly, I should like, on the present occasion, to approach them indirectly and as a group, through a consideration of three influential models of teaching, which provide, or at any rate suggest, certain relevant answers. These models do not so much aim to *describe* teaching as to *orient* it, by weaving a coherent picture out of epistemological, psychological, and normative elements. Like all models, they simplify, but such simplification is a legitimate way of highlighting what are thought

Originally presented as the Marshall Woods Lecture on Education, Brown University, 1964. Variant versions were delivered to the Harvard-Lexington 1964 Summer Program and the Boston University Philosophy Club. Published in *Harvard Educational Review*, Vol. 35 (1965), 131-43. Further discussion of this article appeared in *Harvard Educational Review*, Vol. 35 (1965), 363-7, 492-6. (Copyright 1965 by President and Fellows of Harvard College.)

to be important features of the subject. The primary issue, in each case, is whether these features are indeed critically important, whether we should allow our educational thinking to be guided by a model that fastens upon them, or rather whether we should reject or revise the model in question. Although I shall mention some historical affiliations of each model, I make no pretense to historical accuracy. My main purpose is systematic or dialectical, that is, to outline and examine the three models and to see what, if anything, each has to offer in our own quest for a satisfactory conception of teaching. I turn, then, first to what may be called the 'impression model.'

The impression model

The impression model is perhaps the simplest and most widespread of the three, picturing the mind essentially as sifting and storing the external impressions to which it is receptive. The desired end result of teaching is an accumulation in the learner of basic elements fed in from without, organized and processed in standard ways, but, in any event, not generated by the learner himself. In the empiricist variant of this model generally associated with John Locke, learning involves the input by experience of simple ideas of sensation and reflection, which are clustered, related, generalized, and retained by the mind. Blank at birth, the mind is thus formed by its particular experiences, which it keeps available for its future use. In Locke's words: [1]

> Let us then suppose the mind to be, as we say, white paper, void of all characters, without any ideas: how comes it to be furnished? Whence comes it by that vast store which the busy and boundless fancy of man has painted on it with an almost endless variety? Whence has it all the materials of reason and knowledge? To this I answer, in one word, from experience; in that all our knowledge is founded, and from that it ultimately derives itself. Our observation, employed either about external sensible objects, or about the internal operations of our minds, perceived and reflected on by ourselves, is that which supplies our understandings with all the materials of thinking. These two are the fountains of knowledge, from whence all the ideas we have, or can naturally have, do spring.

Teaching, by implication, should concern itself with exercising the mental powers engaged in receiving and processing incoming ideas, more particularly powers of perception, discrimination, retention, combination, abstraction, and representation. But, more important, teaching needs to strive for the optimum selection and organization of this experiential input. For potentially, the teacher has enormous power; by controlling the input of sensory units, he can, to a large degree, shape the mind. As Dewey remarked,[2]

> Locke's statements ... seemed to do justice to both mind and matter. ... One of the two supplied the matter of knowledge and the object upon which the mind should work. The other supplied definite mental powers, which were few in number and which might be trained by specific exercises.

The process of learning in the child was taken as paralleling the growth of knowledge generally, for all knowledge is constructed out of elementary units of experience, which are grouped, related, and generalized. The teacher's object should thus be to provide data not only useful in themselves, but collectively rich enough to support the progressive growth of adult knowledge in the learner's mind.

The impression model, as I have sketched it, has certain obvious strong points. It sets forth the appeal to experience as a general tool of criticism to be employed in the examination of all claims and doctrines, and it demands that they square with it. Surely such a demand is legitimate, for knowledge does rest upon experience in some way or other. Further, the mind is, in a clear sense, as the impression model suggests, a function of its particular experiences, and it is capable of increased growth with experience. The richness and variety of the child's experiences are thus important considerations in the process of educational planning.

The impression model nevertheless suffers from fatal difficulties. The notions of absolutely simple ideas and of abstract mental powers improvable through exercise have been often and rightly criticized as mythological:[3] simplicity is a relative, not an absolute, concept and reflects a particular way of analyzing experience; it is, in short, not given but made. And mental powers or faculties invariant with subject matter have, as everyone knows, been expunged from psychology on empirical as well as theoretical grounds. A more fundamental criticism, perhaps, is that the implicit conception of the growth of knowledge is false. Knowledge is not achieved through any standard set of operations for the processing of sensory particulars, however conceived. Knowledge is, first and foremost, embodied in language, and involves a conceptual apparatus not derivable from the sensory data but imposed upon them. Nor is such apparatus built into the human mind; it is, at least in good part a product of guesswork and invention, borne along by culture and by custom. Knowledge further involves *theory*, and theory is surely not simply a matter of generalizing the data, even assuming such data organized by a given conceptual apparatus. Theory is a creative and individualistic enterprise that goes beyond the data in distinctive ways, involving not only generalization, but postulation of entities, deployment of analogies, evaluation of relative simplicity, and, indeed, invention of new languages. Experience is relevant to knowledge through providing tests of our theories; it does not automatically generate these theories, even when processed by the human mind. That we have the theories we do is, therefore, a fact, not simply about the human mind, but about our history and our intellectual heritage.

In the process of learning, the child gets not only sense experiences but the language and theory of his heritage in complicated linkages with discriminable contexts. He is heir to the complex culture of belief built up out of innumerable creative acts of intellect of the past, and comprising a patterned view of the world. To give the child even the richest selection of sense data or particular facts alone would in no way guarantee his building up anything resembling what we think of as knowledge, much less his developing the ability to retrieve and apply such knowledge in new circumstances.

A *verbal* variant of the impression model of teaching naturally suggests itself, then, as having certain advantages over the *sensory* version we have just considered: what is to be impressed on the mind is not only sense experience but language and, moreover, accepted theory. We need to feed in not only sense data but the correlated verbal patterning of such data, that is, the *statements* about such data which we ourselves accept. The student's knowledge consists in his stored accumulation of these statements, which have application to new cases in the future. He is no longer, as before, assumed capable of generating our conceptual heritage by operating in certain standard ways on his sense data, for part of what *we* are required to feed into his mind is this very heritage itself.

This verbal variant, which has close affinities to contemporary behaviorism, does have certain advantages over its predecessor, but retains grave inadequacies still, as a model of teaching. To *store* all accepted theories is not the same as being able to *use* them properly in context. Nor, even if some practical correlation with sense data is achieved, does it imply an understanding of what is thus stored, nor an appreciation of the theoretical motivation and experimental evidence upon which it rests.

All versions of the impression model, finally, have this defect: they fail to make adequate room for radical *innovation* by the learner. We do not, after all, feed into the learner's mind all that we hope he will have as an end result of our teaching. Nor can we construe the critical surplus as generated in standard ways out of materials we supply. We do not, indeed cannot, so construe insight, understanding, new applications of our theories, new theories, new achievements in scholarship, history, poetry, philosophy. There is a fundamental gap which teaching cannot bridge simply by expansion or reorganization of the curriculum input. This gap sets *theoretical* limits to the power and control of the teacher; moreover, it is where his control ends that his fondest hopes for education begin.

The insight model

The next model I shall consider, the 'insight model,' represents a radically different approach. Where the impression model supposes the teacher to be conveying ideas or bits of knowledge into the student's mental treasury, the insight model denies the very possibility of such conveyance. Knowledge, it insists, is a matter of vision, and vision cannot be dissected into elementary sensory or verbal units that can be conveyed from one person to another. It can, at most, be stimulated or prompted by what the teacher does, and if it indeed occurs, it goes beyond what is thus done. Vision defines and organizes particular experiences, and points up their significance. It is vision, or insight into meaning, which makes the crucial difference between simply storing and reproducing learned sentences, on the one hand, and understanding their basis and application, on the other.

The insight model is due to Plato, but I shall here consider the version of St Augustine, in his dialogue, 'The Teacher,'[4] for it bears precisely on the points we have dealt with. Augustine argues roughly as follows: the teacher is commonly thought to convey knowledge by his use of language. But knowledge, or rather *new* knowledge, is not conveyed simply by words sounding in the ear. Words are mere noises unless they signify realities present in some way to the mind. Hence a paradox: if the student already knows the realities to which the teacher's words refer, the teacher teaches him nothing new. Whereas, if the student does not know these realities, the teacher's words can have no meaning for him, and must be mere noises. Augustine concludes that language must have a function wholly distinct from that of the signification of realities; it is used to *prompt* people in certain ways. The teacher's words, in particular, prompt the student to search for realities not already known by him. Finding these realities, which are illuminated for him by internal vision, he acquires new knowledge for himself, though indirectly as a result of the teacher's prompting activity. To *believe* something simply on the basis of authority or hearsay is indeed possible, on Augustine's view; to *know* it is not. Mere beliefs may, in his opinion, of course, be useful; they are not therefore knowledge. For knowledge, in short, requires the individual himself to have a grasp of the realities lying behind the words.

The insight model is strong where the impression model is weakest. While the latter, in its concern with the conservation of knowledge, fails to do justice to innovation, the former addresses itself from the start to the problem of *new* knowledge resulting from teaching. Where the latter stresses atomic manipulable bits at the expense of understanding, the former stresses primarily the acquisition of insight. Where the latter gives inordinate place to the feeding in of materials from the outside, the former stresses the importance of firsthand inspection of realities by the student, the necessity for the student to earn his knowledge by his own efforts.

I should argue, nevertheless, that the case offered by Augustine for the prompting theory is not, as it stands, satisfactory. If the student does not know the realities behind the teacher's words, these words are, presumably, mere noises and can serve only to prompt the student to inquire for himself. Yet if they *are* mere noises, how can they even serve to prompt? If they are not understood in any way by the student, how can they lead him to search for the appropriate realities that underlie them? Augustine, furthermore, allows that a person may believe, though not know, what he accepts on mere authority, without having confronted the relevant realities. Such a person might, presumably, pass from the state of belief to that of knowledge, as a result of prompting, under certain conditions. But what, we may ask, could have been the content of his initial belief if the formulation of it had been literally unintelligible to him? The prompting theory, it seems, will not do as a way of escaping Augustine's original paradox.

There is, however, an easier escape. For the paradox itself rests on a confusion of the meaning of *words* with that of *sentences*. Let me explain. Augustine holds that words acquire intelligibility only through acquaintance with reality. Now it may perhaps be initially objected that understanding a word does not always require acquaintance with its signified reality, for words may also acquire intelligibility through definition, lacking such direct acquaintance. But let us waive this objection and grant, for the sake of argument, that understanding a word *always* does require such acquaintance; it still does not follow that understanding a true sentence similarly requires acquaintance with the state of affairs which it represents. We understand new sentences all the time, on the basis of an understanding of their constituent words and of the grammar by which they are concatenated. Thus, given a sentence signifying some fact, it is simply not true that, unless the student already knows this fact, the sentence must be mere noise to him. For he can understand its meaning indirectly, by a synthesis of its parts, and be led thereafter to inquire whether it is, in reality, true or false.

If my argument is correct, then Augustine's paradox of teaching can be simply rejected, on the ground that we *can* understand statements before becoming acquainted with their signified realities. It follows that the teacher can indeed *inform* the student of new facts by means of language. And it further seems to follow that the basis for Augustine's prompting theory of teaching wholly collapses. We are back to the impression model, with the teacher using language not to prompt the student to inner vision, but simply to inform him of new facts.

The latter conclusion seems to me, however, mistaken. For it does *not* follow that the student will *know* these new facts simply because he has been *informed*; on this point Augustine seems to me perfectly right. It is knowing, after all, that Augustine is interested in, and knowing requires something more than the receipt and acceptance of true information. It requires that the student earn the right to his assurance of the truth of the information in question. New *information*, in short, can be intelligibly conveyed by statements; new *knowledge* cannot. Augustine, I suggest, confuses the two cases, arguing in effect for the impossibility of conveying new knowledge by words, on the basis of an alleged similar impossibility for information. I have been urging the falsity of the latter premiss. But if Augustine's premiss is indeed false, his conclusion as regards knowledge seems to me perfectly true: to *know* the proposition expressed by a sentence is more than just to have been told it, to have grasped its meaning, and to have accepted it. It is to have earned the right, through one's own effort or position, to an assurance of its truth.

Augustine puts the matter in terms of an insightful searching of reality, an inquiry carried out by oneself, and resting in no way on authority. Indeed, he is perhaps too austerely individualistic in this regard, rejecting even legitimate arguments from authority as a basis for knowledge. But his main thesis seems to me correct: one cannot convey new knowledge by words alone. For knowledge is not simply a storage of information by the learner.

The teacher does, of course, employ *language*, according to the insight model, but its primary function is not to impress his statements on the student's mind for later reproduction. The teacher's statements are, rather, instrumental to the student's own search of reality and vision thereof; teaching is consummated in the student's own insight. The reference to such insight seems to explain, at least partially, how the student can be expected to apply his learning to new situations in the future. For, having acquired this learning not merely by external suggestion but through a personal engagement with reality, the student can appreciate the particular fit which his theories have with real circumstances, and, hence, the proper occasions for them to be brought into play.

There is, furthermore, no reason to construe adoption of the insight model as eliminating the impression model altogether. For the impression model, it may be admitted, does reflect something genuine and important, but mislocates it. It reflects the increase of the culture's written lore, the growth of knowledge as a public and recorded possession. Furthermore, it reflects the primary importance of conserving such knowledge, as a collective heritage. But knowledge in this public sense has nothing to do with the process of learning and the activity of teaching, that is, with the growth of knowledge in the individual learner. The public treasury of knowledge constitutes a basic source of materials for the teacher, but he cannot hope to transfer it bit by bit in growing accumulation within the student's mind. In conducting his teaching, he must rather give up the hope of such simple transfer, and strive instead to encourage individual insight into the meaning and use of public knowledge.

Despite the important emphases of the insight model which we have been considering, there are, however, two respects in which it falls short. One concerns the simplicity of its constituent notion of insight, or vision, as a condition of knowing; the other relates to its specifically cognitive bias, which it shares with the impression model earlier considered. First, the notion that what is crucial in knowledge is a vision of underlying realities, a consulting of what is found within the mind, is far too simple. Certainly, as we have seen, the knower must satisfy *some* condition beyond simply being informed, in order to have the right to his assurance on the matter in question. But to construe this condition in terms of an intellectual inspection of reality is not at all satisfactory. It is plausible only if we restrict ourselves to very simple cases of truths accessible to observation or introspection. As soon as we attempt to characterize the knowing of propositions normally encountered in practical affairs, in the sciences, in politics, history, or the law, we realize that the concept of a *vision of reality* is impossibly simple. Vision is just the wrong metaphor. What seems indubitably more appropriate in all these cases of knowing is an emphasis on the processes of deliberation, argument, judgment, appraisal of reasons *pro* and *con*, weighing of evidence, appeal to principles, and decision-making, none of which fits at all well with the insight model. This model, in short, does not make adequate room for principled deliberation in the characterization of knowing. It is in terms of such principled deliberation, or the potentiality for it, rather than in terms of simple vision, that the distinctiveness of knowing is primarily to be understood.

Second, the insight model is specifically cognitive in emphasis, and cannot readily be stretched so as to cover important aspects of teaching. We noted above, for example, that the application of truths to new situations is somewhat better off in the insight than in the impression model, since the appropriateness of a truth for new situations is better judged with awareness of underlying realities than without. But a judgment of appropriateness is not all there is to application; habits of proper execution are also required, and insight itself does not necessitate such habits. Insight also fails to cover the concept of character and the related notions of attitude and disposition. Character, it is clear, goes beyond insight as well as beyond the impression of information. For it involves general principles of conduct logically independent of both insight and the accumulation of information. Moreover, what has been said of character can be applied also to the various institutions of civilization, including those that channel cognition itself. Science, for example, is not just a collection of true insights; it is embodied in a living tradition composed of demanding principles of judgment and conduct. Beyond the cognitive insight, lies the fundamental commitment to principles by which insights are to be criticized and assessed, in the light of publicly available evidence or reasons. In sum, then, the shortcoming of the insight model may be said to lie in the fact that it provides no role for the concept of *principles*, and the associated concept of *reasons*. This omission is very serious indeed, for the concept of principles and the concept of reasons together underlie not only the notions of rational deliberation and critical judgment, but also the notions of rational and moral conduct.

The rule model

The shortcoming of the insight model just discussed is remedied in the 'rule model,' which I associate with Kant. For Kant, the primary philosophical emphasis is on reason, and reason is always a matter of abiding by general rules or principles. Reason stands always in contrast with inconsistency and with expediency, in the judgment of particular issues. In the cognitive realm, reason is a kind of justice to the evidence, a fair treatment of the merits of the case, in the interests of truth. In the moral realm, reason is action on principle, action that therefore does not bend with the wind, nor lean to the side of advantage or power out of weakness or self-interest. Whether in the cognitive or the moral realm, reason is always a matter of treating equal reasons equally, and of judging the issues in the light of general principles to which one has bound oneself.

In thus binding myself to a set of principles, I act freely; this is my dignity as a being with the power of choice. But my own free commitment obligates me to obey the principles I have adopted, when they rule against me. This is what fairness or consistency in conduct means: if I could judge reasons differently when they bear on my interests, or disregard my principles when they conflict with my own advantage, I should have no principles at all. The concepts of *principles, reasons,* and *consistency* thus go together and they apply both in the cognitive judgment of beliefs and the moral assessment of conduct. In fact, they define a general concept of rationality. A rational man is one who is consistent in thought and in action, abiding by impartial and generalizable principles freely chosen as binding upon himself. Rationality is an essential aspect of human dignity and the rational goal of humanity is to construct a society in which such dignity shall flower, a society so ordered as to adjudicate rationally the affairs of free rational agents, an international and democratic republic. The job of education is to develop character in the broadest sense, that is, principled thought and action, in which the dignity of man is manifest.

In contrast to the insight model, the rule model clearly emphasizes the role of principles in the exercise of cognitive judgment. The strong point of the insight model can thus be preserved: the knower must indeed satisfy a further condition beyond the mere receiving and storing of a bit of information. But this condition need not, as in the insight model, be taken to involve simply the vision of an underlying reality; rather, it generally involves the capacity for a principled assessment of reasons bearing on justification of the belief in question. The knower, in short, must typically earn the right to confidence in his belief by acquiring the capacity to make a reasonable case for the belief in question. Nor is it sufficient for this case to have been explicitly taught. What is generally expected of the knower is that his autonomy be evidenced in the ability to construct and evaluate fresh and alternative arguments, the power to innovate, rather than just the capacity to reproduce stale arguments earlier stored. The emphasis on innovation, which we found to be an advantage of the insight model, is thus capable of being preserved by the rule model as well.

Nor does the rule model in any way deny the psychological phenomenon of insight. It merely stresses that insight itself, wherever it is relevant to decision or judgment, is filtered through a network of background principles. It brings out thereby that insight is not an isolated, momentary, or personal matter, that the growth of knowledge is not to be construed as a personal interaction between teacher and student, but rather as mediated by general principles definitive of rationality.

Furthermore, while the previous models, as we have seen, are peculiarly and narrowly *cognitive* in relevance, the rule model embraces *conduct* as well as cognition, itself broadly conceived as including processes of judgment and deliberation. Teaching, it suggests, should be geared not simply to the transfer of information nor even to the development of insight, but to the inculcation of principled judgment and conduct, the building of autonomous and rational character which underlies the enterprises of science, morality and culture. Such inculcation should not, of course, be construed mechanically. Rational character and critical judgment grow only through increased participation in adult experience and criticism, through treatment that respects the dignity of learner as well as teacher. We have here, again, a radical gap which cannot be closed by the teacher's efforts alone. He must rely on the spirit of rational dialogue and critical reflection for the development of character, acknowledging that this implies the freedom to reject as well as to accept what is taught. Kant himself holds, however, that rational principles are somehow embedded in the structure of the human mind, so that education builds on a solid foundation. In any event, the stakes are high, for on such building by education depends the prospect of humanity as an ideal quality of life.

There is much of value in the rule model, as I have sketched it. Certainly, rationality is a fundamental cognitive and moral virtue and as such should, I believe, form a basic objective of teaching. Nor should the many historical connotations of the term 'rationality' here mislead us. There is no intent to suggest a faculty of reason, nor to oppose reason to experience or to the emotions. Nor is rationality being construed as the process of making logical deductions. What is in point here is simply the autonomy of the student's judgment, his right to seek reasons in support of claims upon his credibilities and loyalties, and his correlative obligation to deal with such reasons in a principled manner.

Moreover, adoption of the rule model does not necessarily exclude what is important in the other two models; in fact, it can be construed quite plausibly as supplementing their legitimate emphases. For, intermediate between the public treasury of accumulated lore mirrored by the impression model, and the personal and intuitive grasp of the student mirrored by the insight model, it places general principles of rational judgment capable of linking them.

Yet, there is something too formal and abstract in the rule model, as I have thus far presented it. For the operative principles of rational judgment at any given time are, after all, much more detailed and specific than a mere requirement of formal consistency. Such consistency is certainly fundamental, but the way in which its demands are concretely interpreted, elaborated, and supplemented in any field of inquiry or practice, varies with the field, the state of knowledge, and the advance of relevant methodological sophistication. The concrete rules governing inference and procedure in the special sciences, for example, are surely not all embedded in the human mind, even if the demands of formal consistency, as such, *are* universally compelling. These concrete rules and standards, techniques and methodological criteria evolve and grow with the advance of knowledge itself; they form a live tradition of rationality in the realm of science.

Indeed, the notion of tradition is a better guide here, it seems to me, than appeal to the innate structure of the human mind.

Rationality in natural inquiry is embodied in the relatively young tradition of science, which defines and redefines those principles by means of which evidence is to be interpreted and meshed with theory. Rational judgment in the realm of science is, consequently, judgment that accords with such principles, as crystallized at the time in question. To teach rationality in science is to interiorize these principles in the student, and furthermore, to introduce him to the live and evolving *tradition* of natural science, which forms their significant context of development and purpose.

Scholarship in history is subject to an analogous interpretation, for beyond the formal demands of reason, in the sense of consistency, there is a concrete tradition of technique and methodology defining the historian's procedure and his assessment of reasons for or against particular historical accounts. To teach rationality in history is, in effect, here also to introduce the student to a live tradition of historical scholarship. Similar remarks might be made also with respect to other areas, e.g., law, philosophy and the politics of democratic society. The fundamental point is that rationality cannot be taken simply as an abstract and general ideal. It is embodied in *multiple evolving traditions*, in which the basic condition holds that issues are resolved by reference to *reasons*, themselves defined by *principles* purporting to be impartial and universal. These traditions should, I believe, provide an important focus for teaching.

Conclusion

I have intimated that I find something important in each of the models we have considered. The impression model reflects, as I have said, the cumulative growth of knowledge in its *public* sense. Our aim in teaching should surely be to preserve and extend this growth. But we cannot do this by storing it piecemeal within the learner. We preserve it, as the insight model stresses, only if we succeed in transmitting the live spark that keeps it growing, the insight which is a product of each learner's efforts to make sense of public knowledge in his own terms, and to confront it with reality. Finally, as the rule model suggests, such confrontation involves deliberation and judgment, and hence presupposes general and impartial principles governing the assessment of reasons bearing on the issues. Without such guiding principles, the very conception of rational deliberation collapses, and the concepts of rational and moral conduct, moreover, lose their meaning. Our teaching needs thus to introduce students to those principles we ourselves acknowledge as fundamental, general, and impartial, in the various departments of thought and action.

We need not pretend that these principles of ours are immutable or innate. It is enough that they are what we ourselves acknowledge, that they are the best we know, and that we are prepared to improve them should the need and occasion arise. Such improvement is possible, however, only if we succeed in passing on, too, the multiple live traditions in which they are embodied, and in which a sense of their history, spirit, and direction may be discerned. Teaching, from this point of view, is clearly not, as the behaviorists would have it, a matter of the teacher's shaping the student's behavior or of controlling his mind. It is a matter of passing on those traditions of principled thought and action that define the rational life for teacher as well as student.

As Professor Richard Peters has written,[5]

> The critical procedures by means of which established content is assessed, revised, and adapted to new discoveries have public criteria written into them that stand as impersonal standards to which both teacher and learner must give their allegiance... To liken education to therapy, to conceive of it as imposing a pattern on another person or as fixing the environment so that he 'grows,' fails to do justice to the shared impersonality both of the content that is handed on and of the criteria by reference to which it is criticized and revised. The teacher is not a detached operator who is bringing about some kind of result in another person which is external to him. His task is to try to get others on the inside of a public form of life that he shares and considers to be worthwhile.

In teaching, we do not impose our wills on the student, but introduce him to the many mansions of the heritage in which we ourselves strive to live, and to the improvement of which we are ourselves dedicated.

Notes

1 *Essay Concerning Human Understanding.* Book II, Chap. 1, Sect. 2.
2 John Dewey, *Democracy and Education*, New York: Macmillan, 1916, p. 72.

3 Dewey, *ibid.*, '... the supposed original faculties of observation, recollection, willing, thinking. etc., are purely mythological. There are no such ready-made powers waiting to be exercised and thereby trained.'

4 J. Quasten and J. C. Plumpe (eds), *Ancient Christian Writers*, No. 9, St Augustine, 'The Teacher,' translated and annotated by J. M. Colleran, Westminster, Maryland: Newman Press, 1950; relevant passages may also be found in Kingsley Price, *Education and Philosophical Thought*, Boston: Allyn & Bacon, 1962, pp. 145-59.

5 *Education as Initiation*, London: Evans; an inaugural lecture delivered at the University of London Institute of Education, 9 December 1963.

7 University scholarship and the education of teachers

What are the ingredients of a teacher's education? The question is old and controversial, surely not to be settled in the space of an essay. Yet certain of its philosophical aspects may perhaps profitably be explored in brief compass, and it is such aspects that I wish to treat here, especially as they relate to the general role of university scholarship in the preparation of teachers.

This latter theme has, I believe, been relatively underplayed in contemporary treatments of the question. Recent educational reforms have largely addressed themselves to the proper structuring of subject matter and its articulation in the teaching process. Discussion of the teacher's education has tended accordingly to concern itself, not with the general strengthening of his powers through scholarly studies, but rather with improving his grasp of the particular subject to be taught and providing him with practical experience in its classroom presentation.

In earlier days, there was also, to be sure, much confident talk of a putative science of education. The first annual convention of American normal-school principals in 1859, for example, passed a resolution proclaiming that 'education is a science.' Richard Edwards, later president of Illinois Normal University, protested in vain on that occasion that sciences are built not by proclamation but by research.[1] Yet even he was convinced that research would yield such a science, of fundamental importance in the training of teachers. In 1865, he declared:[2]

> It is not, I trust, necessary, at this late day, to assure you that there is here as noble a science as ever engaged the thought of man. There are immutable principles here, that ought to be studied and comprehended by every young person entering upon the work of teaching. There is, in the nature of things, a foundation for a profession of teachers.

The development of a distinctive science of education has not,

A preliminary version was presented at the Fall Orientation Meetings of the Harvard Graduate School of Education in 1967. Published in *Teachers College Record*, Vol. 70 (1968), 1-12; reprinted by permission of the publisher.

however, come about, and with increasing rejection of the idea of such a science in recent years,[3] there has been a growing tendency to exalt either specific subject-matter competence or classroom practice into a position of primacy in the preparation of teachers, with moderates striving, as ever, for an even balance between the two.

My own view is that the whole framework of this latter discussion has been too constricted, and that the preparation of teachers in a university setting, in particular, offers the special opportunity to develop a broader conception. Beyond a teacher's knowledge of his subject and his practice in the art of teaching under supervision, he needs to be helped, I am convinced, to relate his work in suitable manner to the family of scholarly and research disciplines represented by the university at large.[4]

Nor does such a conviction imply a return to the fruitless quest for a distinctive science of education as a foundation for the teaching profession. There is indeed, I believe, little to support the faith that such a distinctive science will one day be developed. The belief that the profession requires such a science as its foundation is, however, misguided. For if there be no distinctive science or special discipline of education, there are surely multiple modes of analyzing educational problems in a scientific spirit and a disciplined manner.[5] The teacher's preparation should lead him to relate his own tasks to such modes, and teacher education should thus be an integral undertaking of the whole university.

The underlying point was well put by the American philosopher Josiah Royce in 1891. Arguing against the conception of education as a science, Royce insisted nevertheless that 'the undertakings of pedagogy' are 'capable of scientific and general discussion.'[6] Indeed, there is, he wrote, 'no science of education. But what there is, is the world of science furnishing material for the educator to study,' offering 'aid from the scientific spirit and counsel from scientific inductions.'[7] It is, I suggest, the family of university studies, representing the world of science and the material of general discussion, that needs to be brought to bear on the teacher's work. I am, of course, not arguing for some particular administrative arrangement. Alternative arrangements are compatible with the general idea of initiating the teacher into disciplined perspectives, scholarly and humanistic, from which his professional work may be viewed.

To set forth such a general idea is in itself, however, hardly to persuade. Indeed, doubts are encountered almost immediately upon reflection. What is the point of a scholarly emphasis in the education of teachers? asks the skeptic in each of us. Can an initiation into disciplined analyses of education really be thought necessary for effective teaching? What is the use of theoretical sophistication that is not translatable into subject-matter competence or strengthened practical skills? Have we not all known teachers of power and resourcefulness, innocent of educational history and philosophy, ignorant of psychology and the social sciences, and yet capable of transmitting their subjects effectively to the minds of their students? Is not the emphasis on scholarly disciplines then merely an eccentricity natural to scholars or, worse still, a fraudulent attempt to give education the aura of professionalism? So speaks the skeptic, and he deserves a serious answer, for he raises questions fundamental to any philosophy of teaching. Let me, then, sketch the sort of reply I am myself inclined to give to his challenge.

In general, though I hold the skeptic's doubts to be searching and important, I believe they flow from faulty reasoning. Consider his stress on what is necessary for effective teaching, indeed his appeal to such presumed necessity as a criterion for evaluating the education of teachers. By this criterion, he implies, we must admit the importance of subject-matter competence and practical training. For, surely, without a knowledge of the subject to be taught, and without practical classroom procedures mastered through experience, a man cannot teach effectively; justification is thus conceded to these ingredients in the preparation of teachers. However, continues the skeptic, application of the same necessity criterion serves to exclude the ingredient of scholarly sophistication, since effective teaching may perfectly well proceed without an initiation into critical and disciplined approaches to the educational process. Such approaches, he concludes, therefore have no justification in the preparation of teachers.

From the reasonable premiss that whatever is necessary for effective teaching is thereby justified as an element of training, the skeptic has invalidly concluded that *only* what is thus necessary can be justified. He has, in effect, exalted necessity into a unique position and ruled out all other principles of justification. Such exclusion is, however, quite vulnerable on general grounds. For by parallel reasoning one might argue, for example, that shock absorbers and automatic transmissions ought to be done away with since they are not essential to effective transportation, that carpets and paintings have no legitimate place in the home because they do not contribute to effective shelter, that literature and the fine arts are unjustified as civilized pursuits because unnecessary to sustain life.

Surely, the skeptic's attitude is too reductive. Justification is not, as he supposes, simply a matter of minimal necessity. It is rather, a matter of desirability, and a thing may be desirable not because it is something we could not do without, but because it transforms and enhances the quality of what we do and how we live. If a justification is needed for the teacher's scholarly and theoretical sophistication regarding his work, it is not that, lacking it he cannot manage to teach, but that having it, the quality of his effort and role is likely to be enhanced. It is a maximal rather than a minimal interpretation of the teacher's work that is thus relevant to a philosophical assessment of his education.

In what, however, does such an enhancement of quality as has been mentioned consist? What are its concrete manifestations? How, specifically, does it show itself if, while inessential to mastery of the subject to be taught, it is also, by hypothesis, not transmuted into practical skill or improved maxims of classroom procedure? Does not theory, in general, refine the operations of craft through developing its technology? Is not a theoretical study of education therefore exposed as utterly irrelevant to the practice of teaching if it fails to foster new devices and specialized procedures for the conduct of schooling? Here is a further, and a persuasive, challenge of the skeptic.

It should first be noted, however, that an important concession underlies this new challenge. The earlier complaint against a theoretical ingredient in the teacher's education was that it was not required for effective teaching. Now it seems to be allowed that such an ingredient might be independently justified, after all, as advancing the technology of education. Though the individual teacher does not require theoretical sophistication in order to perform his own work effectively, such sophistication may, it is now suggested, facilitate the invention of new methods and techniques, with a resultant improvement in the general state of the art. The skeptic therefore implicitly grants a place to theory provided it promises to yield technological improvements in educational practice. Against all other theory he is adamant.

One difficulty in this new position of the skeptic is that there is no sure way of telling in advance if, when, or how a bit of theoretical sophistication will transform practice. If he interprets his new doctrine so liberally as to admit all basic theory that might conceivably yield practical change, he virtually abandons his opposition altogether. On the other hand, if he is to maintain effective opposition to specified bodies of theoretical content on the ground that they do not presently seem to him technologically promising, he cannot provide a principled basis for his judgment that will be generally acceptable to others, and he runs the real risk, moreover, of excluding technologically fruitful material. In sum, if the skeptic's present criterion is to avoid being simply vacuous, it must run the risk of being applied in a manner that is arbitrary and shortsighted, even from a techno-logical point of view.

There is, however, a more fundamental reply that needs to be made to the present challenge of the skeptic. For he may argue that, although there is no generally acceptable, principled basis for estimating technological promise in advance, there is at least a rough intuitive ranking of theories that can be made, with respect to their relative promise. And he may add that, while some risk is admittedly involved in excluding theories beyond a certain designated point in the ranking, such a risk is inevitable in all estimation, and is well worth taking, here as elsewhere, in order to facilitate the making of practical decisions.

The more fundamental reply hinges then, not on the problem of applying the skeptic's present criterion, but rather on the criterion's basic concept of technological promise. For the skeptic construes the import of theory in education as consisting wholly in its power to transform the technology of teaching through pro-viding new maxims of procedure. Educational improvement is seen as consisting altogether in a refinement of the teacher's operations in the pursuit of his craft. It is this implicit assimila-tion of educational improvement to technological development that I believe to be inappropriate, for the reduction of the teacher's role to the set of operations performed by him is, in fact, impossible.

It has, indeed, become increasingly fashionable in recent years to construe the teacher's work as that of[8]

a minor technician within an industrial process, the overall goals ... [of which are to be] set in advance in terms of national needs, the curricular materials prepackaged by the disciplinary experts, the methods developed by educational engineers—and the teacher's job ... just to supervise the last operational stage, the methodical insertion of ordered facts into the student's mind.

The trouble with this picture is that it is radically wrong, both normatively and descriptively. The teacher, in a free society at least, is not just a technician, but also one of the shapers of the educational process. Moreover, he influences students not only through his activity, but by his identity.

In the paradigmatic case of industrial design and manufacture, the technician operates upon inert materials; he does things to these materials under the guidance of rules improvable through investigation and experiment. These materials are shaped by what he thus does; they are not responsive to what he is. They react to what is done to them by the technician but they do not enter into communication with him. They do not, in the process of their own shaping into output, question his judgments and beliefs, his perspectives and purposes. They present him with no new centers of personal experience, by relating to which his own meanings may be engaged and transformed.

Teaching is, in every crucial respect, vastly different. Although the teacher's procedures are also subject to improvement through scientific research and experiment, the student is not mere inert material to be worked on by rule. He enters into communication with the teacher and, through the teacher, with the heritage of culture common to both. Such communication broadens and refines the student's initial outlook, and thereby increases his understanding.

But the process is not onesided, for in the student's efforts to understand, he questions and explores, doubts and evaluates. And he thus responds not only to the explicit material of the lesson but to its larger ramifications, not only to what the teacher does, but also to what he intends and represents. He is, in short, alive not simply to the content of classroom activities but to the manner in which they are carried out, the standards and convictions they reflect, and the larger rationale that underlies them. The teacher is, moreover, committed to honoring the student's quest for understanding by providing him with honest answers; that is to say, answers he himself finds genuinely compelling. The teacher is thus called upon to reveal, and hence to risk, his own judgments and loyalties in the process of teaching others. In embracing this risk, the teacher is himself forced to a heightened self-awareness, and a more reflective attitude toward his own presuppositions; his own outlook is thereby broadened and refined.

For the teacher to conceive his role after the analogy of industrial production is, then, I believe, a distorting fallacy of far-reaching consequence. His role is not reducible to the operations he performs; it draws heavily upon his capacities for insight into his own principles and allegiances. And it demands an ability to reflect critically on these principles and allegiances in the face of the searching curiosity of the young.

His preparation for teaching is thus strengthened not simply through an increased mastery of procedures, but through a development of his resources for carrying on a significant conversation with the young; that is to say, through a widening of his intellectual perspectives, a quickening of his imaginative and critical powers, and a deepening of insight into his purposes as a teacher and the nature of the setting in which these purposes are pursued. Do not scholarly and theoretical studies of educational problems find sufficient justification in the rich opportunities they offer for such a strengthening of the teacher's resources?

But perhaps, it will be thought, the skeptic rejects any such appeal to 'cognitive' rather than 'operational' notions, in the process of justification. Being a skeptic, he is after all professionally hardheaded; he does not look with favor upon concepts of insight, reflection, and intellectual perspective, nor does he relish elusive references to a strengthening of the teacher's resources. He recognizes the importance of mastery of the subject to be taught, and the significance of reliable classroom procedures. But any appeal to a notion of latent intellectual power he finds obscure and therefore unacceptable.

To this line of thought there are, it seems to me, two replies. The skeptic's general aversion to nonoperational concepts is, in the first place, not decisive in countering the specific arguments previously offered. If these arguments are sound, they cast doubt on the operational bias motivating the very aversion in question. To insist that the arguments must be wrong simply because they clash with the aversion would be to beg the question.

In the second place, the skeptic must himself acknowledge a principle of justification that ranges beyond what can be reflected in operational maxims of the classroom. For, let us remind him, he has spoken glibly of the necessity of knowledge of a subject for effective teaching. And what, we may ask him, is a subject? Is history, for example, a subject? Surely, effective teaching of a given history lesson or course does not require a general knowledge of history, as such. Nor does effective teaching of a particular topic in mathematics require a knowledge of mathematics, taken as a whole. Nor, finally, does effective teaching of a particular English poem or literary period require a comprehensive mastery of English literature. The boundaries of the subject in every case reach far beyond the scope of the teacher's actual classroom work. If knowledge of the subject is nevertheless justified in the skeptic's eyes, he has implicitly, and despite his vaunted hardheadedness, granted the importance of a nonoperational ingredient in the teacher's preparation.

Now it may, perhaps, be objected that this latter reply to the skeptic takes for granted the standard everyday concept of a subject. Subject-matter rubrics, it will rightly be said, are crude practical devices of grouping that are variable at will. Mathematics need not be construed so expansively as to embrace all mathematical topics, nor should history be interpreted as covering the whole sweep of human events, when we are concerned with the particular problem of specifying the education of teachers. In dealing with this problem we are, in every case, that is, presupposing a narrower conception of the relevant subject to be mastered by the teacher.

This conclusion, though correct, is not, however, sufficient to save the skeptic from implicit appeal to a nonoperational component in the teacher's education. For the skeptic, no matter how narrowly he conceives the subject-matter preparation of the teacher, does not, in practice, construe any subject so narrowly as to collapse it into the single course nor, certainly, into the single lesson being taught for the day. Whatever he means by insisting on the necessity of a knowledge of the subject, the subject represents, for him, too, a wider circle of materials and instrumentalities surrounding the content to be taught, access to which strengthens the teacher's powers and, in so doing, heightens the possibilities of his art. Though it does not translate itself uniformly into technological improvement, it is acknowledged, even by the skeptic, to be justified as an ingredient of the teacher's education.

And once such a notion is admitted, can we put bounds to it? Can we say: 'This much surrounding matter represents an important teaching resource, but beyond this nothing significant is to be found'? How difficult such a position would be! Indeed, to recognize that the ordinary notion of a subject is artificial should lead us rather to break its pervasive hold over our educational conceptions. Subjects should be taken to represent, not hard bounds of necessity which confine the teacher's training, but centers of intellectual capacity and interest radiating outward without assignable limit. Anything that widens the context of the teacher's performance, whether it extends his mastery of related subject matter or, rather, his grasp of the social and philosophical dimensions of his work, has a potential contribution to make to his training. It is in the latter respects particularly that scholarly and theoretical studies of education find their proper rationale.

Thus far, in replying to the skeptic, I have addressed myself mainly to the notion of justification, the import of theory, and the nature of subjects. A last, but by no means unimportant, aspect of the skeptic's doctrine that remains to be discussed is his emphasis on effective teaching. For, as we have seen, he considers the effective practice of teaching to constitute a basic focus of relevance in evaluating the teacher's preparation. One question that should, however, be raised concerns the clarity of the general idea. Is teaching effectiveness so clear a notion that it can perform properly in the fundamental evaluative role thus assigned to it?

No matter how we initially understand it, I think we must agree, upon reflection, that evaluating the effectiveness of teaching is not a simple thing. Any serious attempt to assess such effectiveness raises not only difficult practical questions of inquiry and measurement but also fundamental issues concerning reasonable criteria of judgment. What qualities of classroom performance and what influences on the students should enter into a judgment of effectiveness?

Turning first to classroom performance, it is important to stress the subtlety and delicacy of the teacher's interchange with the student. A crude demand for effectiveness easily translates itself into a disastrous emphasis on externals simply because they are easier to get hold of than the central phenomena of insight and the growth of understanding. In an important essay of 1904,[9] John Dewey distinguished between the inner and outer attention of children, the inner attention involving the 'first-hand and personal play of mental powers' and the outer 'manifested in certain conventional postures and physical attitudes rather than in the movement of thought.' Children, he noted, 'acquire great dexterity in exhibiting in conventional and expected ways the *form* of attention to school work.' The 'supreme mark and criterion of a teacher,' according to Dewey, is the ability to bypass externals and to 'keep track of [the child's] mental play, to recognize the signs of its presence or absence, to know how it is initiated and maintained, how to test it by results attained, and to test *apparent* results by it.' The teacher 'plunged prematurely into the pressing and practical problem of keeping order in the schoolroom,' Dewey warned, is almost of necessity going 'to make supreme the matter of external attention.' Without the reflective and free opportunity to develop his theoretical conceptions and his psychological insight, he is likely to 'acquire his technique in relation to the outward rather than the inner mode of attention.'[10] Effective classroom performance surely needs to be judged in relation to the subtle engagement of this inner mode, difficult as it may be to do so.

Let us look now at the question of influence on the students, as a component of teaching effectiveness. What sorts of influence are relevant? Is the students' knowledge of material alone to be considered, or shall we also take into account their problem-solving capacity, their attitudes, their propensity for inquiry, the hidden alteration of their perceptions and sensibility which may become manifest, if at all, only long after they have left the classroom? Even the hard knowledge of material is not, despite the confidence of the test-makers, a simple thing to gauge or analyze. William James's comments of nearly eighty years ago are still fresh and instructive on this topic.[11]

> We are all too apt to measure the gains of our pupils by their proficiency in directly reproducing in a recitation or an examination such matters as they may have learned, and inarticulate power in them is something of which we always underestimate the value. The boy who tells us, 'I know the answer, but I can't say what it is,' we treat as practically identical with him who knows absolutely nothing about the answer at all. But this is a great mistake. It is but a small part of our experience in life that we are ever able articulately to recall. And yet the whole of it has had its influence in shaping our character and defining our tendencies to judge and act. Although the ready memory is a great blessing to its possessor, the vaguer memory of a subject, of having once had to do with it, of its neighborhood, and of where we may go to recover it again, constitutes in most men and women the chief fruit of their education. This is true even in professional education. The doctor, the lawyer, are seldom able to decide upon a case off-hand. They differ from other men only through the fact that they know how to get at the materials for decision in five minutes or half an hour: whereas the layman is unable to get at the materials at all...
>
> Be patient, then, and sympathetic with the type of mind that cuts a poor figure in examinations. It may, in the long examination which life sets us, come out in the end in better shape than the glib and ready reproducer, its passions being deeper, its purposes more worthy, its combining power less commonplace, and its total mental output consequently more important.

To take James's words seriously is to realize how complex and subtle is the notion of effectiveness in teaching; how far from providing a firm educational criterion marking an end, rather than an opening, of inquiry and reflection.

The main point to which I would here call attention is, however, a different one. It concerns not the clarity of the notion of teaching effectiveness, but rather the implied emphasis on the teaching performance, in contrast with the role of the teacher.

How indeed is this role itself to be understood? Is the teacher to be thought of as an intellectual technician, whose teaching performance may be more or less effective by whatever criteria of value and of influence may be chosen, but who has no voice in setting these criteria? Or is he, on the contrary, to be thought of as a man with a calling or vocation committing him to the values of truth, reason, and the enlargement of human powers, dedicated to raising his voice for them, and to shaping the conditions of his work so that these values may flourish? His effectiveness as a teacher, in the light of the latter conception, is quite different from the restricted notion of his effectiveness in classroom performance.

The skeptic's emphasis on effectiveness in teaching is, I should argue, too narrow, for it leads him to conceive teacher training as geared primarily to the refinement of performance, and to underestimate the significance of the teacher's larger role. A society aspiring to be genuinely free cannot afford such a restricted view. It must appreciate, indeed insist on, the fundamental relevance of enlightenment and critical thought in all matters bearing on the nurture of its cultural life. It needs, in particular, to view its teachers not simply as performers professionally equipped to realize effectively any goals that may be set for them. Rather, it should view them as free men and women with a special dedication to the values of the intellect and the enhancement of the critical powers of the young.

In such a role, teachers cannot restrict their attention to the classroom alone, leaving the larger setting and purposes of schooling to be determined by others. They must take active responsibility for the goals to which they are committed, and for the social setting in which these goals may prosper. If they are not to be mere agents of others, of the state, of the military, of the media, of the experts and the bureaucrats, they need to determine their own agency through a critical and continual evaluation of the purposes, the consequences, and the social context of their calling.

If we accordingly conceive of the education of teachers not simply as the training of individual classroom performers, but as the development of a class of intellectuals vital to a free society, we can see more clearly the role of educational scholarship and theoretical analysis in the process. For, though the latter do not directly enhance craftsmanship, they raise continually the sorts of questions that concern the larger goals, setting, and meaning of educational practice. It is these questions that students need continually to have before them as they develop into mature teachers, if they are indeed to help shape the purposes and conditions of education. To link the preparation of teachers with such questions is the special opportunity of the university.

The family of studies and disciplines represented by the university is not, let us be clear on this, a happy family. It harbors quarrels and nasty feuds as well as sweetness and light. But the contribution it offers to teacher education presupposes neither an unattainable coherence of perspectives nor an artificial consensus on details. It consists rather in an enlargement of the intellectual context within which a teacher views his work. Such an enlargement centers the work within a web of new relationships, altering its familiar outlines and inviting novel perceptions of its import. In so doing, it continually suggests alternatives to encrusted assumptions, generating insistently larger questions of meaning, setting, and purpose. In its shared commitment to critical thought and responsible inquiry, moreover, the family of scholarly studies spurs the teacher's effort to attain a more rational insight into his task. It is the quest for such insight, within ever-growing contexts of meaning, that frees the teacher and fits him to teach free men.

Notes

1 See Merle L. Borrowman, *Teacher Education in America : A Documentary History*, New York: Columbia University, Teachers College Press, 1965, p. 74.

2 Richard Edwards, 'Normal Schools in the United States,' *Lectures and Proceedings*, National Teachers' Association, 1865: reprinted in Borrowman, *op. cit.*, p. 80.

3 See related discussions of the question of an educational discipline in John Walton and James L. Kuethe, *The Discipline of Education*, Madison, Wisconsin: University of Wisconsin Press, 1963. (See, in particular, 'Is education a discipline?' reprinted as Chap. 4 in the present volume.)

4 See related discussions in *The Graduate Study of Education : Report of the Harvard Committee*, Cambridge: Harvard University Press, 1966.

5 See Chap. 4 above.

6 Josiah Royce, 'Is There a Science of Education?', *Educational Review*, 1, (Jan., Feb. 1891); reprinted in Borrowman, *op. cit.*, p. 107.

7 *Ibid.*, pp. 126-7.

8 I. Scheffler, 'Concepts of Education: Some Philosophical Reflections on the Current Scene,' in Edward Landy and Paul A. Perry, eds, *Guidance in American Education: Backgrounds and Prospects*, Cambridge: Harvard Graduate School of Education [distributed by Harvard University Press], 1964, pp. 22-3; reprinted as Chap. 5 in the present volume.

9 John Dewey, 'The Relation of Theory to Practice in Education,' National Society for the Scientific Study of Education, *The Relation of Theory to Practice in the Education of Teachers*, 3rd Yearbook, Part I (Bloomington, Ill.: Public School Publishing, 1904); reprinted in Borrowman, *op. cit.*

10 Dewey, in Borrowman, *ibid.*, pp. 148-9.

11 William James, *Talks to Teachers on Psychology; and to Students on Some of Life's Ideals*, New York: Norton, 1958, Chap. 12, pp. 100-1.

Educational content

Part 3

Science, morals and educational policy

8

Introduction

To recognize that education is a practical art is not merely to acknowledge the triviality that it is an activity or process, but more significantly, to class it among those undertakings with dominant objectives, capable of indefinite refinement through increasing grasp of underlying principles. While the single instance always involves intuitive judgment in applying appropriate principles, as well as in coping with features whose governing principles are yet unknown, the promise of progress in arts like medicine, psychiatry, engineering, communication, and education lies in research into underlying principles, i.e., in a scientific understanding of the phenomena in question, their conditions, relations, and outgrowths. This importance of science as a systematic basis for the educator's art does not, however, exhaust its relevance for education. For a significant part of the *content* of education, i.e., what the educator wishes to transmit to learners, consists precisely of scientific information and scientific modes of thought and understanding. Science may, then, be adjudged a vital ingredient in both method and content in educational practice.

Since it is thus doubly important to the educator, it would seem imperative that he have a clear grasp of its functions, uses, and limits. Yet the interpretation of science is generally so fraught with confusion that such understanding is not easy to attain, and educational discussions are consequently often misled at crucial points by pseudo-issues. Perhaps the prime example concerning educational method is the lingering dispute between 'scientists'

Parts of this paper were presented to the Harvard 1954 Summer School Conference on 'Science and Educational Policy.' It was prepared, in substantially its present form, for the Committee on Curriculum Exploration of the Harvard Graduate School of Education in 1955, and appeared in *Harvard Educational Review*, Vol. 26 (1956), 1-16. (Extracts from *Philosophy in American Education*, ed. Charles W. Hendel *et. al.*, Harper & Row, 1945.) Reprinted by permission of President and Fellows of Harvard College.

and 'humanists,' in the very formulation of which lurk crucial confusions between scientific modes of inference, scientific techniques, and scientifically grounded technology, usually ignored by both parties. The 'scientific' side thus often exaggerates its case by arguing for the universal relevance of some limited technique or technology, while the 'humanist' side feels pushed into denying that educational results have conditions which can be studied systematically and, in effect, that education can be rationally planned, while it simultaneously advances (contradictory) claims for some preferred educational program as calculated to lead most efficiently to desired objectives. This dispute lacks logical substance because it rests on insufficiently analyzed notions of science.

An equally familiar example concerning content rather than method is the problem of objectives in science education. Once it is granted that some more general aim is involved than the acquisition of current scientific information, the problem of delimiting it precisely begins, and the inevitable complexity of this inquiry is quite often needlessly magnified by confusions over 'scientific method.' Those favoring scientific method as the *general* aim of science instruction often confuse it with the temporal order of a good many inquiries in the sciences, e.g., from problem to hypothesis to testing, etc., or with some technique, e.g., experiment or measurement. Those who (rightly) point out that the latter are limited and by no means universally applicable often go on to reject inductive, empirical modes of inference altogether in favor of intuition, inertia, or dogma. At bottom, there is again a failure to make relevant distinctions in the analysis of science. In view of the educational importance of such analysis, it is hoped that the following sections, devoted to selected issues in the interpretation of science bearing on education, may be of some use.

Can science be applied to education?

This question ostensibly cuts to the roots of issues of educational method. If science is applicable to human teaching and learning, both can be increasingly understood and improved by well-known modes of investigation and control. If not, we must either resign ourselves to current levels of educational insight and practice or call in a totally new approach to learning phenomena. As a matter of fact, the question may be viewed as part of a more general dispute as to whether or not social subject matter requires a radically different method of inquiry from that used in the natural sciences.

Yet, as just stated in general form, the issue between 'differentists' and 'uniformists' is hopelessly muddled. For in some sense, methods of inquiry differ even *within* the natural sciences, and indeed, from problem to problem within any given science. It will be quickly argued, however, that this is not the sense in which differentists intend their claim for a radically new method in social inquiry, nor that in which uniformists deny it. The former affirm some *radical* difference in the two realms, relative to which internal differences are slight, while the latter affirm a radical uniformity, overshadowing undeniable differences in approach and technique. But how radical must a difference be to be a *radical* difference, and how basic must a uniformity be to qualify as *really* basic? If the issue is not to degenerate into a mere verbal quibble as to whether to include or exclude social studies in the application of the term 'science,' uniformists and differentists must specify *in advance* just those aspects of method relative to which their respective claims of uniformity and difference are intended.

Reconstructing the issue most plausibly in some such terms, we may distinguish in specified ways between *logical method* and *technique* within the natural sciences and ask whether the former is or is not applicable to social studies as well. By *logical method* we may understand, e.g.:

(1) Formulation of assertions in logically coherent, objectively testable systems of hypotheses.
(2) Observational control of the acceptance and rejection of assertions.
(3) Inductive or probabilistic interpretation of observational evidence.
(4) Theoretical reversibility of all decisions on acceptance and rejection of assertions.
(5) Use of general hypotheses and singular statements to explain and predict occurrences.

By *technique* we may understand any features of scientific work but these, e.g., apparatus, modes of observation or data-collection. Uniformists may now be construed as claiming that the above characteristics of method apply equally to social sciences, while differentists deny this claim.

Even with this reconstruction, however, the issue may be wrongly understood, since it is surely not of the same order as the verbally similar question, 'Does glue apply equally well to glass as to paper?', or 'Does this statute apply equally to minors?' The latter are relatively easy to answer by gathering and validly interpreting easily attainable empirical evidence. The issue of logical method, on the other hand, concerns the range of the very standards governing valid empirical inference. Past successes in employing such inference in natural science cannot be taken as evidence for success in social studies without begging the question. Past successes in the social studies may constitute partial evidence only if we grant the validity of these principles in determining such successes, and such evidence is often disputed in detail. The important point here, however, is that prior evidence of success is not necessary as a justification of social science, just as prior evidence of success is unnecessary and indeed impossible, as a justification of induction generally in the natural sciences. What sufficiently justifies our presumption to abide by given norms of logical method is the fact that they adequately codify our accumulated store of accepted inferences and our intuitive conceptions of acceptable inferences. That the principles above listed do so for these inferences irrespective of social or non-social content is, then, the minimal sufficient claim of uniformists. Differentists, on the other hand, have generally offered specific reasons for limiting the scope of these principles to nonsocial subject matter.

So interpreted, the issue rests on the validity of the latter reasons, since the very fact that differentists feel it necessary to advance such special arguments for limiting the scope of the above principles means that they recognize the general claim of the latter on our acceptance. Once we examine these special differentist arguments in detail, it becomes clear, I think, that they have no force at all and that they present no convincing reasons for limiting the scope of logical method, as above defined, to nonsocial subject matter. An exhaustive analysis is, of course, out of place here, but a short survey of some typical arguments follows, together with comments on what I conceive to be their fatal weaknesses in each case.

(a) *Uniqueness*—social sciences deal with unique occurrences; hence objective test by different investigators at different positions in space or time is impossible, while general hypotheses are excluded by the same token, thus making it theoretically impossible to predict. [Every occurrence, however, is unique in some sense, while for any two occurrences, some property is common to both.]

(b) *Historicity*—social sciences aim to achieve historical knowledge, not general laws; hence explanation and prediction in a scientific sense are impossible. [But geology and astronomy are directly historical in part, physics rests on historical evidence embodied in particular reports, while all three employ general principles in arguing from and reconstructing historical material. Even cultural history must use general principles in interpreting data; unless it did it could not, e.g., weight relevance of historical factors and construct a 'historically explanatory' account.]

(c) *Value-character*—social subject matter is value-impregnated; hence objectivity is theoretically impossible. [But to study values, we need neither to espouse them nor reject them any more than to study the law of falling bodies we need to jump from the Tower of Pisa. In any event, scientific objectivity means not lack of values or interests, but rather their frank exposure and tentative espousal, and the institutionalizing of procedures for submitting valued hypotheses to test by investigators with counter-interests.]

(d) *Selective focus*—social scientists, especially historians, select their material, thus precluding objectivity. [But selection, on the level of choice of problem, is unavoidable even in the natural sciences; only selection in the sense of arbitrary avoidance of relevant evidence is pernicious. But why is *such* selection inevitable in the social sciences?]

(e) *Social bias*—social class position of social scientist must bias his findings and render them subjective. [But bias, in the sense of selective observation, is inevitable everywhere, e.g., physical and physiological status of observer biases his perceptual perspective. The very distinction between biased and unbiased observation allows theoretical possibility of correction for biases by specific devices in each case. Only bias in the sense of arbitrary repudiation of counter-evidence is bad, but why is this an inevitable concomitant of social study, in view of the fact that it is *logically possible* for a social bias and counter-opinion to co-occur? Finally, what is the status of this argument itself, if we accept it; is it merely a function of social class?]

(f) *Need for intuitive empathy*—study of human motivations, passions, and needs requires empathy, *verstehen*, intuitive insight, rather than projection of tentative hypotheses with subsequent public confirmation. [But intuitive insights do not in themselves constitute adequate justifications for acceptance of beliefs, since they are often in mutual conflict.

They are at best *sources* of hypotheses, and as such occur equally in the natural sciences, but in this role require rather than preclude subsequent public test. Finally, we may hypothesize without prior sympathetic insight; few of us can empathize with Hitler, yet we might be reasonably said to understand and explain his behavior.[1]]

(g) *Impossibility of experiment or measurement*—no controlled experiments or measurement can be made in the social studies, thus precluding objectivity. [But this is surely false for some areas in social study, while no controlled experiments are conducted in geology or astronomy and measurement is of little importance in, e.g., branches of biology, geology. Controlled experiment and measurement are techniques logically independent of method as above defined, and surely unnecessary for objectivity.]

(h) *Complexity*—social phenomena are much more complex than natural phenomena; hence cannot be studied by above logical method at all. [But prior to Galileo, physical subject matter was thought complex, since its principles were unknown. Is the point of this argument perhaps that physics cannot explain social phenomena? But neither can social study explain physical phenomena. Is it rather that physical assumptions and controls enter into social investigations? But analogous assumptions about the observer must be made in physical investigations. Is the point that while physical things are completely explained by physics, social objects are not? But not all aspects of physical things are explained by current physics, unless we trivially redefine 'physical things' to mean just those aspects so explained, or trivially reinterpret the claim so as to mean by 'physics' whatever does explain physical things completely.]

To reject these and analogous differentist arguments does not, of course, necessitate denying that the current state of social study is in a much more primitive state than physical science, but it does mean that there is no theoretical barrier to the advance of scientific study of social phenomena, and in particular, of education. There are, to be sure, practical problems to overcome, devices of control and correction to be invented, and much theoretical ingenuity required to extend such study, but these are obstacles very like the ones to be met everywhere in scientific research. Theoretically, science *can* be applied to education.

Has science failed modern culture?

The present question raises considerations of a different order. It is now no longer a matter of deciding for or against the *possibility* of a social science. Rather, the issue becomes the *desirability* of a social science. In the present context of war and worldwide tension, in which scientific information has played a key role, it is perhaps possible to understand the qualms of those who would reject scientific thought altogether. It is, however, not so easy to make sense of attempts to transform these qualms into rational arguments. A consideration of some of these attempts may prove instructive.

(a) The simplest argument from modern culture against the desirability of science asserts that it is the *cause* of our present social ills: if there were no highly developed physics, no advanced engineering, no technological progress in the arts of propaganda, the present world crisis would be unthinkable. As generally offered, this argument treats logical method, technique, and technology on a par (thus confusing scientific thought and its uses), but it can easily be reformulated so as to refer solely to logical method in research inasmuch as it is indispensable to technical development. It may also be readily admitted that the present social situation would indeed be inconceivable without the widespread use of scientific methods of investigation.

The difficulty resides in the fact that this point establishes only that science is a *necessary* condition for our current social situation with its various evils. Aside from the fact that it might, by analogous evidence, be shown to be a necessary condition also for the various goods we enjoy, the crucial point is that a condition may be necessary for a given effect E without being sufficient to produce it. Now 'cause' is a quite ambiguous notion generally, but we would ordinarily not wish to denote as cause of E a condition C which might, within appropriate contexts, occur without E, i.e., one that is insufficient for E. Thus, though the widespread use of scientific modes of investigation is indeed indispensable for modern culture, it is hardly the *cause* of modern culture or its ills. To judge otherwise, on the grounds of its being a *necessary* condition, would mean equally our attributing causal efficacy to the fact that we have, e.g., digestive systems, language, opposable thumbs, or to the fact that the sun is neither too hot nor too cold to support life on the earth, etc., since each of these conditions is equally indispensable to the state of our culture. Like the latter factors, scientific modes of thought are insufficient to produce current culture while indispensable to much beside its evils which we value, i.e., rational inference.

Culture is a product not alone of its necessary but of its prior sufficient set of conditions, comprising much more than the use of scientific modes of understanding, e.g., political and economic organization, social customs and traditions, individual and collective choices, etc. Scientific modes of investigation contribute to the constant refinement of empirical information, and hence, by increasing the potential effectiveness of our choices, weight those choices with increasing moral responsibility. But they are not sufficient to *determine* either our choices or the resultant complex patterns of behavior we call culture. We need not, to better society, advocate anything so absurd as abandoning our reason.

(b) Often a weaker but more sophisticated argument from culture is offered against the desirability of scientific investigation, especially into social phenomena. Here it is no longer asserted that science is the *cause* of our social evils, but rather that it has been shown impotent to remove them, as evidenced by the fact that they are still with us. But why should this in itself justify abandoning scientific investigation? The presence of social evils shows equally, by analogous argument, that every other actual aspect of our culture has been impotent to remove them. Whereas these other aspects are taken to be justified nevertheless, e.g., often as ends worthwhile in themselves, some critics treat the justification of scientific thought as resting solely on its alleged promise to better society.

A little reflection will show, however, that this alleged promise is an inadequate criterion for the justification of science, not simply because other criteria may turn out equally or more relevant, but because the promise itself makes no sense. Scientific investigation can, when successful, yield information concerning the empirical conditions of phenomena, but this is independent of the practical problem of *instituting* such conditions in a particular case. Thus, e.g., the information that John Jones's cure depends on his taking medicine may be scientifically validated, and moreover true, whether or not he actually decides to take his medicine. If he refuses and consequently dies, his heirs cannot legitimately blame his physicians. If they insist, 'But you promised to cure him!' the sufficient retort is, 'We promised *contingent* on his following our advice in instituting conditions known to be sufficient for his cure.' In short, when the scientist states sufficient conditions C for an event E, he is at best only contingently 'promising' E. Whether or not C occurs is a matter of fact dependent (in practically every case) on all sorts of factors outside of the scientist's actual utterance, and perhaps in the most interesting instances, on cultural choices. If E fails to occur, this need prove nothing more than that C failed to occur. An absolute promise of E, irrespective of conditions other than the scientist's utterance, would be incantation not science. The scientist's alleged promise to better society is, thus, at best a conditional one, contingent on instituting appropriate initial conditions; it is in itself no *prediction* of these initial conditions, and cannot be falsified by their failure to occur.

In the previous section, we were concerned to show that science is not a sufficient, but rather a necessary, causal condition for our current social situation and its evils. What we have here been saying amounts to an analogous denial that science is a sufficient causal condition for social progress. To judge it unfavorably because it has not accomplished what it cannot accomplish is patently absurd. Scientific thought is a necessary condition for the extension of planned action in control of the future, and this in itself is justification of its desirability, unless we are willing to give up extending planned activity altogether. Even if we were, we might still acknowledge the inherent worthwhileness of the scientific search for understanding of the world.

(c) One final set of comments must be devoted to a widespread argument against science on alleged grounds of its cultural divisiveness. Science, it is said, in becoming increasingly specialized, corrodes the unity of culture; in eternal questioning, it undermines the common values on which society rests. Our need is for integration rather than technical specialization, and so we must, in one way or another, restrict the scope of scientific modes of understanding and investigation. Much thinking of this sort appears to underlie the current movement in general education (which, however, need not stand or fall with this argument).

There is, certainly, a real practical problem posed by the proliferation of subjects, areas of investigation, and information recently developed in the sciences, and hence, especially in education, a real need for some explicit over-all map to aid individuals in orienting themselves in the world of current ideas. But the very urgency of this need should make us more, not less, critical of current demands for educational 'order' and 'integration,' so that we may be less swayed by rhetoric than by a clear-sighted view of the merits of each proposal.

The first step in this direction, it seems to me, is the recognition that order and integration are, in the abstract, neither absolute goods nor evidences of truth. As Professor C. J. Ducasse has put the matter: [2]

> The education provided in the medieval universities at their best is sometimes held up as an example of education ordered by unifying principles. But these were, or rested on, a set of religious dogmas then generally accepted. These dogmas had the status of articles of faith rather than of facts scientifically established, and some of them are widely questioned today. They did provide a basis for order in education, but order is not by itself a guarantee of truth or of worth, since error, folly and tyranny can also be systematized and institutionalized, and indeed have to be so if they are to maintain themselves.
>
> On the other hand, lack of order or unity can mean—and in our colleges today doubtless does in part mean—that the horizon of values acknowledged has so broadened, and the harvest of facts discovered and of powers acquired become so rich, that time has not yet sufficed to integrate all this adequately in thought and practice. But, plainly, the remedy does not lie in so contracting this horizon and so ignoring or belittling this harvest that only so much of what they offer is kept as can be fitted into some authoritarian synthesis elaborated earlier. Rather, what wisdom commands is to put the best resources of constructive imagination, or rational, open-minded experimentation, and of sympathy with natural human aspirations to work at the task of formulating a philosophy of life and of education that will do justice to all aspects of the picture as we discern it today.

Second, it is perhaps well to recall the educational benefits of *disintegration* in one basic sense. It is a fact of life that the modes of experience are various and that they generate differing perspectives, norms, and sensibilities. It is, it seems to me, an educational experience of the highest value to be confronted with these differences at an appropriate age, and to learn at first hand the disjointednesses and incongruities which no administrative integration can forever hide. Even within any one domain, say a particular science, it is highly desirable, I think, for the student to learn that the opinions and approaches of experts differ violently, that the community of truth-seekers is not just one happy family, but that truth is born precisely out of their quarrels and clashes, their individual and often disrespectable *aperçus*. A student who gets all his education screened through some neat integrative framework imposed in advance by others, without being forced to make his own sense of the discordances and discrepancies patent in experience, has been effectively protected from thinking altogether.

Nor is the case against specialization *per se* as strong as some critics make out. Specialization is not just an unfortunate quirk of scientists; it is a corollary of the precision and reliability of empirical information garnered by modern modes of investigation. Neither is specialization anything new essentially: Aristotle and St Thomas were nothing if not specialists in a highly refined technique. In every craft, art, job, and profession, achievement has always been conditioned on attention to details, special practice, technical mastery. Modern science is not revolutionary in demanding specialization; its novelty lies rather in directing this demand toward a new set of problems—discovering the empirical relationships among phenomena. To oppose specialization *as such* is to oppose not merely science but excellence.

And indeed, proponents of the argument under discussion usually turn out to be advocating not simply that specialization, *in the abstract*, be replaced by order, *in the abstract*, but rather that specialization be encouraged only in restricted areas, within a framework of order. It often appears, further, that this order needs to be unquestioned and taught as such if it is to 'support' the common values of social life. But the underlying premiss of this view—that specialization is naturally antithetical to cultural 'unity,' and that eternal questioning is incompatible with common values—is absurd. The model apparently projected by proponents of this view, if I may be permitted a metaphor here, is that of an overarching framework or shell to contain or encase variation within fixed limits. What is overlooked, to extend this metaphorical description, is the possibility of unity through internal structure, a unity that would not set fixed limits to variation but would infuse it as it varied. It is the latter unity that characterizes the community of scientific investigators precisely while they specialize and question, a unity of logical method and accepted criteria of criticism[3] rather than a unity of fixed doctrine. If there were not this kind of structural unity of critical method, special findings could never be understood and employed elsewhere even within science nor would criticism and dispute over these findings make sense. Far from precluding unity, scientific specialization presupposes commonly accepted canons of inference. The eternal questioning of scientists with a view toward subjecting every doctrine to the widest possible test *is itself* a common value in science. To call for another kind of unity to be achieved by limiting this questioning or specialized investigation in a fixed way is to sacrifice science, and needlessly at that. For democratic social organization has precisely the same rationale—a unity based not on common, unquestioned social dogma, but rather on common methods of dealing with specialized interests and claims, and the eternal questioning of every such claim (even the claim for democracy) as itself a unifying value.

Nevertheless, would not a deliberate over-all picture of the realms of knowledge be helpful in the orientation of learners? This notion of structural unity suggests perhaps one way to meet the real practical problem in education of providing students with a map of special areas and information, without some dogmatic integrative scheme to supplement specialization from without and to limit scientific questioning. This way would be teaching not merely to transmit skills and conclusions within every area, but also to make *explicit* each domain's structural unity, the canons of judgment and inference appropriate to each. For the sciences, e.g., this would involve getting across not simply results, but modes of inference by which any empirical findings are supported. This does not, incidentally, mean sacrificing precision and talking in generalities, for precision itself is a general scientific ideal embedded in the structure of scientific inference. It does mean, however, making explicit the canons of judgment involved in reaching particular findings. If the goal of general or liberal education is orientation within the world of ideas, a map of areas based on canons of judgment would seem to be one good way of realizing this goal.

The teaching required for this approach would, it may incidentally be suggested, need to be of a much broader type than that needed to train practitioners. The practitioner needs to know his area only from within, so to speak, and to *use* the common canons of the domain. The teaching here envisaged would need to make *explicit* these canons, and to compare the whole domain to others; it would need, i.e., to look at the domain from above and from the outside as well as from within. To use S. Toulmin's terms,[4] such teaching would need to employ *onlooker's* as well as *participant's* language to explain the rationale of a field of study. If teaching at its best, even for practitioners, should be of this sort, it would seem that a broader understanding is generally required for teaching than for practice in any given field, i.e., an explicit map of the field both structurally and in its relations to others, as well as an ability to *operate effectively* within it.

Must a science of education deny man's freedom?

The problem of free will is an old one, yet its capacity to puzzle and confuse seems not to diminish with the years. Briefly, it is this: moral concepts seem to require free will. There is no sense in holding someone responsible for an act that he was forced to do or that occurred by accident; he must have been free to choose or to avoid committing any act for which he is praised or blamed. On the other hand, the scientist's major goal is to discover the empirical conditions of all phenomena, including human behavior. Now, to the extent that he is successful in determining these conditions, he is showing that such behavior is a natural product of antecedent factors, and hence not free at all. Is the scientist's major goal, then, incompatible with the meaningfulness of moral experience?

If we (especially as educators) once accept the notion of such incompatibility, we are bound to end up with paradox. We may, e.g., assert the view[5] that since man is regarded as the product of forces outside himself, he can no longer be regarded as free, responsible, or creative, and that the educator's task is to recognize this fact and frankly aim at controlling the behavioral outcomes of learners entrusted to his care. This opinion fails to explain our clear use of moral notions and our distinction between acts which the agent is free to choose and all others. At the same time, it appears to deny that we do not as educators wish to control learners so much as to enable them to become self-sufficient and emancipated from our temporary control in the learning situation. Alternatively, we may grasp the other horn of our apparent dilemma and affirm that since moral choices are patently free, human behavior must be undetermined or unpredictable in a way that makes the goal of science unreasonable in application to man's affairs. This view fails to explain the generality with which the principles of logical method in empirical inquiry (discussed above) appeal to us, nor can it deny evidence already accumulated concerning the dependence of features of behavior on selected factors of genetic history and environment. Educationally, this position is, in a practical sense, intolerable since, if educational outcomes are unpredictable (hence uncontrollable), we can neither warrantably plan educational programs nor warrantably criticize any in terms of their consequences.

Fortunately, we need not exclude either the meaningfulness of moral notions or the deterministic goals of a science of human affairs, since their alleged incompatibility is a myth based on the fallacy of equivocation; the associated puzzle over the nature of educational control is moreover seen to be equally specious once attention is called to the equivocal use of the term 'control.'

(a) The clarification of the general problem of free will has been often and repeatedly accomplished in philosophical writings and commands unusual consensus among philosophers.[6] It consists generally in distinguishing two meanings of 'free': (1) An act A is said to be free relative to its performer X, if it is (sufficiently) a causal product of X's choice (rather than of factors independent of such choice, e.g., external coercion or accident, etc.). (2) An act A is said to be free if it is uncaused altogether. Let us hereafter distinguish these two senses by using 'voluntary' for the first and 'uncaused' for the second.

Note first, now, that these two senses do not simply diverge but are incompatible inasmuch as an uncaused act can be no causal product and hence must be nonvoluntary while voluntary acts cannot be uncaused. Note, secondly, that it is freedom in the sense of voluntariness which is required for the application of moral concepts, not freedom in the sense of uncausedness. If an act A is really uncaused, it is no more attributable to its performer's choice than to any other antecedent condition and it would be senseless to hold him *responsible for* it. Nor, incidentally, if his choice were itself uncaused, would it make sense to praise or blame him with the hope of influencing his choice of behavior in the future. Only if choice contributes to the determination of an act and is itself at least partially determinable by social factors does it make sense to attribute responsibility and apply social sanctions which may, in affecting choice, indirectly influence action. Where we have reason to believe that a given act was forced upon an agent against his will or was accidental or beyond his control, we do not judge him morally for it. Nor, when we have reason to believe that moral sanctions will be less effective than some other method (e.g., in the case of mental illness) in influencing choice, will we morally judge the agent, at least to the same degree. In no event is uncausedness *required* for explaining our use of moral concepts, but rather excluded to the extent that these concepts apply.

To sum up, the scientist's goal of exhibiting the causal background of human behavior is not at all incompatible with freedom in the only morally relevant sense. To take either paradoxical horn of our previous dilemma results from confusing two senses of 'free' and is completely unnecessary. Far from denying responsibility, indeed, the increase of scientific knowledge, by rendering our choices more effective, makes us more responsible morally for our behavior.

(b) If the confusion over free will is anthropomorphic in mistaking causation for coercion, an analogous anthropomorphism pervades the equivocal use of 'control' responsible for our previous paradox. The paradox, it will be remembered, was this: as the science of human behavior advances, the educator's ability to control the learning process increases. But the more he exercises this ability, the more he violates our moral judgment that his duty is not to control his students but rather to enable them to outgrow his temporary control. To the extent, however, that he takes this moral judgment seriously by denying the possibility of an advancing science of human behavior, or by refusing to apply accumulated information to educational policy, he denies that educational outcomes are subject to control and hence that he can rationally plan or criticize educational programs in the light of their empirical consequences.

Is the efficient educational use of an advancing human science incompatible, then, with our conception of the duties of the educator? An affirmative answer based on the above considerations would anthropomorphically confuse two distinct senses of 'control': (1) One *person* X is said to control *another* Y if (in relevant respects) Y's behavior is subject to X's directions or commands, i.e., Y is obedient to X. (2) A *person* X is said to control a *phenomenon* P if he can intentionally produce (and avert) the causal conditions for P. Call the first sense 'personal dominance' and the second 'causal planning.'

Regarding these two senses, notice first that while X may achieve personal dominance without causal planning, he may causally plan to achieve personal dominance. Note, second, the crucial point that X may causally plan without personal dominance; indeed he may causally plan to relinquish personal dominance: to foster *dis*obedience. These senses, then, while not incompatible, are nevertheless independent. Note, finally, that while science enhances the educator's ability to control the *phenomena* of learning, i.e., to *causally plan* them, he may exercise this ability, if he desires, to foster criticism, independence, disobedience, rebelliousness, etc., while our moral judgment against his *personal dominance* over students in no way involves a rejection of causal planning as such. Indeed to make this judgment really effective, we should need to causally plan for the withering away of whatever temporary dominance is required in the formal learning situation.

In sum, we need not reject but should rather welcome the

Science, morals and educational policy

possibility of applying science to education in order to realize our moral notion of the educator's job. Nor, in welcoming this possibility are we *ipso facto* committed to the extension of personal dominance; the crucial moral option remains open for the educator of applying science to foster not a stultifying obedience and conformity but rather critical mentality, personal integrity, and moral independence. To the extent that these qualities do not magically pop in and out of existence at random but are lawfully conditioned on empirical antecedents, to that extent the scientific discovery of such antecedents will be educationally valuable.

Is science morally neutral?

In the previous discussion, we have tangentially touched on issues concerning relations of science to value. We have denied that scientific thought is a sufficient causal condition either for general social evil or social progress, while affirming that it is a necessary component of rational planning, inasmuch as such planning involves inductive inference about the conditions of phenomena. But while it is thus itself justifiable by reference to the objective of rational planning, and while as a component of the latter it admittedly enables us to judge the relative adequacy of alternative means to given objectives of various sorts, does it have no more positive import for value problems? Can it, that is, serve as a *guide* in deciding moral choices, in choosing not only planning *techniques* but planning *objectives*? Or is it only a valuable, even indispensable tool, but one that can be used either wisely or wickedly, i.e., compatibly with *any* set of objectives?

Before approaching this question directly, it seems to me fruitful to distinguish two relevant senses of 'science' in terms of which it might be posed: (A) Science as a system of sentences warranted by appropriate canons of method and formulating available information, (B) Science as a complex set of cultural behavior-patterns involving research, communication, and publication activities directed toward producing adequate systems of sentences in the sense of (A). Let us now interpret our question with reference to each of these senses.

If, with (A), we consider science as *a set of sentences*, we must admit, at the outset, its logical compatibility with any *activity*, moral or immoral. Or, rather, we must deny the applicability of the notion of 'logical compatibility' here altogether, since the latter applies between *sentences or sets of sentences* exclusively. This is, however, a trivial result for it holds even for value-statements proper, e.g., a man may *affirm* 'kindness is good' and *act* cruelly without breach of *logic*.

We may more reasonably interpret our question here as asking if every acceptable value-*statement* is reducible to an acceptable scientific one, i.e., if value-statements are translatable into scientific statements whose truth or falsity can be correctly decided by familiar methods. This is a difficult and highly controversial question on which current philosophy is sharply divided. It seems to me that there is no advance reason why this question should not turn out answerable in the affirmative, and I think that specific philosophic arguments purporting to demonstrate such reasons are mistaken.[7] Nevertheless, it cannot be gainsaid that no universally accepted reduction is presently available or that fundamental disagreement exists even among philosophic analysts sympathetic to the idea of reduction.

It seems to me, however, that much more can be presently said relative to our question interpreted with reference to (B). Here again there can be no issue of logical incompatibility since we are now considering science as a complex of activities. But there surely is such a thing as empirical incompatibility between activities which, as a matter of fact, exclude or tend to exclude each other. To decide for a given activity means that we must decide against activities incompatible with it if we want our decisions to be jointly capable of fulfillment.[8] A joint positive decision on empirically incompatible activities is not logically invalid but is pragmatically inconsistent, i.e., self-defeating.

Now, there is perhaps wider agreement on scientific activity as an objective than on many other social issues (as well as on philosophical justifications of science). But the support and extension of such activity, culturally institutionalized, is *not* empirically compatible with all other activities, e.g., it is incompatible with the suppression of free communication and publication, with political control of belief on scientific questions, with low educational level, etc. Scientific *findings* may indeed be used for totalitarian, authoritarian, and aggressive purposes, but only at the cost of the ultimate restriction or decay of science as a set of *cultural practices*. Science, then, is not pragmatically consistent with *every* set of cultural objectives and cannot in this sense be considered morally neutral; its fate is bound up with that of freedom in social organization. It is no accident that the rise of modern totalitarianisms and totalitarian tendencies is accompanied by a severe political caging of scientific endeavor, to leave room for a dogmatic social rationale backed by the force of the state. Once we look at science as a human activity rather than a set of doctrines, and shift our attention from divergent *justifications of science as a means,* to what science *justifies as a widely cherished end,* we discover an important sense in which science *can* guide us in moral choice. The prevalent picture of science as an efficient, morally neutral tool (even if it is right as regards (A), which is by no means certain) is blind to the wide normative force of scientific behavior as an ideal, as well as to its empirical conditions and outgrowths as an element of culture.

We have previously mentioned some ways in which a broader approach is required for teaching than for practice in a given field. What has here been said, if correct, indicates a further respect in which science teaching in particular might profitably be broadened, at least on some levels of instruction, viz., by getting across some awareness of the moral implications of scientific behavior. It goes without saying that the methods of doing this may vary and none need be directly incorporated into courses in the special sciences. But there should, it seems to me, be increased emphasis on research in the sociology and history of science at an advanced level and as an integral part of science specialization and general courses on the secondary level as well. To map the relations of the sciences not only among themselves but to problems of cultural and moral choices would help provide the general orientation so widely felt as a real need.

Notes

1 I am indebted for certain of my comments in this and the preceding few paragraphs to Professor Ernest Nagel, 'The Logic of Historical Analysis,' in Feigl and Brodbeck, eds, *Readings in Philosophy of Science,* New York: Appleton-Century-Crofts, 1953. Those who want a more extended treatment of related issues should consult Professor Nagel's excellent discussion.

2 *Philosophy in American Education,* New York: Harper, 1945, p. 121.

3 See, e.g., F. Kaufmann, *Methodology of the Social Sciences,* New York: Oxford University Press, 1944. See also Professor Sidney Hook's various papers on the philosophy of democracy.

4 S. Toulmin, *Philosophy of Science,* New York: Hutchinson University Library, 1952.

5 B. F. Skinner, *Science and Human Behavior,* New York: Macmillan, 1953, Chap. 29.

6 See C. L. Stevenson, *Ethics and Language,* New Haven: Yale

University Press, 1944, Chap. 14, and 'The Freedom of the Will,' in *Knowledge and Society*, by the University of California Associates, New York: Appleton-Century, 1938; reprinted in Feigl and Sellars, eds, *Readings in Philosophical Analysis*. Variation in terminology, emphasis, and detail is, naturally, to be expected with different treatments.

7 See I. Scheffler, 'Antinaturalist Restrictions in Ethics,' *Journal of Philosophy* (July 1953). For an attempt at a naturalistic interpretation see also I. Scheffler, 'On Justification and Commitment,' *Journal of Philosophy* (March 1954).

8 For a discussion of 'entailed decisions,' see H. Reichenbach, *The Rise of Scientific Philosophy*, Berkeley: University of California Press, 1951, p. 288.

9

Justifying curriculum decisions

Decisions that confront educators are notoriously varied, complex, and far-reaching in importance, but none outweighs in difficulty or significance those decisions governing selection of content. In view of recent talk of 'teaching children rather than subject matter,' it is perhaps worth recalling that teaching is a triadic relation, describable by the form '*A* teaches *B* to *C*,' where '*B*' names some content, disposition, skill, or subject. If it is true that no one teaches anything unless he teaches it to someone, it is no less true that no one teaches anybody unless he teaches him something.

We do not, moreover, consider it a matter of indifference or whim just what the educator chooses to teach. Some selections we judge better than others; some we deem positively intolerable. Nor are we content to discuss issues of selection as if they hinged on personal taste alone. We try to convince others; we present ordered arguments; we appeal to custom and principle; we point to relevant consequences and implicit commitments. In short, we consider decisions on educational content to be responsible or justifiable acts with public significance.

If these decisions are at once inescapable, important, and subject to rational critique, it is of interest to try to clarify the process of such critique, to state the rules we take to govern the justifying of curricular decisions. Such clarification is not to be confused with an attempt to justify this or that decision; rather, the aim is to make the grounds of decision explicit. Furthermore, clarification cannot be accomplished once and for all time but is rather to be seen as a continuing accompaniment to educational practice.

It is the task of clarification that I shall consider here. I shall

---

Originally prepared for the Committee on Curriculum Exploration of the Harvard Graduate School of Education in 1957. Published in *School Review*, Vol. LXVI (1958), 461-72. (Copyright 1958 by the University of Chicago.) The discussion of justification is based on my article 'On Justification and Commitment,' *Journal of Philosophy*, Vol. LI (1954), 180-90.

offer an analysis of the process of justification along with suggestions for justifying decisions on curriculum.

What is subject to justification? A child may be asked to justify his tardiness, but he would never be asked to justify his cephalic index. Fiscal policies and choices of career are subject to justification, but typhoons and mountain ranges are not. Justifiability applies, it seems, only to controllable acts, or *moves*, as they will henceforth be called.

In this respect, justifiability is paralleled by the notion of responsibility, with which indeed it is intimately related. If I am held responsible for violating a traffic regulation, I expect to be subject to the demand that I justify my violation. Conversely, the child who is called on to justify his late arrival for dinner is being held responsible for his tardiness. The child may escape the need to justify his lateness by denying his responsibility for it. He can deny his responsibility by denying that his lateness was a move at all, by claiming that it could not be helped, was not deliberate or subject to his control.

Now that I have asserted that only moves are justifiable, I must immediately add one qualification. In ordinary discourse, we do not limit justifiability to moves. A city-planning group may debate the justifiability of a projected highway. However, the issue here can ultimately be construed as the justification of moves calculated to produce the highway in question. In general, ostensible reference to the justifiability of non-moves may be construed as a shorthand reference to the justifiability of moves appropriately related to non-moves. Where such moves are lacking, the justification of non-moves fails to arise as an issue. Thus, while we may speak of highways and courses of study as justifiable, we do not inquire into the justification of comets or rainbows. Justifiability may, then, be taken as a universal property of moves; and those that are, in fact, justified comprise a subclass of moves with a certain authority in our conduct.

How are moves justified? If the justified moves represent a subclass of all moves, then to justify a particular move requires that we show it to be a member of this subclass. If no further specification of this subclass is given, we have a relative sense of justification.

Consider chess: we have a board and the standard pieces. We understand what constitutes a move, and we have rules that permit only certain moves. These rules, in effect, define a subclass of all moves. For a player to justify his move as a chess move requires that he show that it belongs to the chess subclass. Such justification is strictly limited, for it depends clearly on the set of rules that define chess. There are an indefinite number of other rule-sets singling out alternative subclasses of moves. A move justified for chess may not be justified for checkers and vice versa. A chess player justifying his move is not implying that chess is superior to checkers. He is only showing that his move conforms to the rules of chess. Hence we cannot speak, strictly, of a move on the board as justified in general or in the abstract; we have to specify also the operative rules.

Some processes of justification resemble the justification of moves in chess and in other formal games. These processes have a well-specified set of rules defining appropriate moves. Justification consists in showing that a move conforms to these rules, that is, belongs to the subclass singled out by them. There is no thought of justifying the set itself as against alternatives. Though it may not be explicitly stated, it is evident that moves are being justified only relative to this set. These conditions seem to apply when, for example, we consider Smith's driving on the right side of the road (in Massachusetts) to be justified. Driving on the right conforms to Massachusetts traffic rules. We are by no means claiming that these rules are unique or superior to alternative rules; for example, rules of countries where driving on the left is prescribed. What is involved here is relative justification. Traffic regulations are, in an important sense, like chess rules or games in general. For one reason or another we may be interested for the moment in playing a certain game or in seeing what the game demands in a particular case. But the existence of alternative games fails to upset us, nor is the comparative justification of the games as such in question.

Relative justification is not limited to such clear cases as traffic control. Much of our conduct falls within the range of less well-defined rules, or social practices and traditions. Much of the time, we justify this conduct simply by appeal to conformity with established practice. Nor should it be supposed that such justification is always as uncomplicated as that of our traffic illustration. Often a move is justified by appeal to a rule, and that rule by appeal to another. For example, Smith's right-hand driving may be justified by a demonstration of its conformity with Massachusetts law and this particular law by conformity with traditional legal practice throughout the United States. Though various levels are distinguishable, it is still true that the justification as a whole is here carried out in relation to American practice. That is, such practice sanctions a class of certain subclasses of moves, one subclass of which includes the move in question. In effect, one 'game' is justified by showing its embed-dedness in another, larger 'game.'

The relative sense of justification is, however, not exhaustive of the types of justification that one uses and, in itself, is hardly satisfactory for many purposes, since every move is both justified and unjustified in relation to appropriately chosen sets of rules. If I am not, as in a game, asking what move I ought to make in order to comply with some particular set of rules, but am asking what move I ought to make at all, the relative sense of justification will be of no help whatever. At best, it can lead me to an-other query of the same sort on a new level and leave me equally undecided there. The nonrelative, or general, request for justifi-cation is, furthermore, one we often make or imply, and in the most important departments of life—belief, social relations, in-dividual choices.

When we decide broad educational issues, we are often asking not merely what jibes with American practice, past or present, but what is generally justified, whether or not it is sanctioned by practice. The desire to evade this general question is understand-able because it is difficult. But this evasion, I think, is responsible for much of the inadequacy of value-discussions in education. Two tendencies seem to develop. A move is defended on grounds of its conformity with American practice, and the question of the justification of this practice itself is not considered at all. Or it is flatly asserted that it is the duty of the teacher to conform to the educational practices of his society, an assertion that, besides calling on a nonrelative notion of duty that is itself uncriticized, seems to many schoolmen to be far from obvious.

Both the nature of this general request for justification of acts or moves and the possibilities for dealing with it may be illumi-nated by comparison with belief. To know that a belief is justi-fied in relation to certain evidence does not provide general justification unless we have confidence in the evidence to begin with. With this initial confidence or credibility, we can proceed to provide ground for our belief. Roughly speaking, what we seem to do is to justify beliefs that not only hang together logically but also, as a family, preserve this initial credibility to the highest degree. We judge belief in question by its general impact on all other beliefs in which we have some confidence. No matter how confident we are of a particular belief, we may decide to give it up if it conflicts with enough other beliefs in which we have a higher degree of confidence.

In practical situations, of course, we do not actually take all our beliefs into account. We concern ourselves, rather, with a limited domain of beliefs that we feel are interdependent. Furthermore, we do not make piecemeal estimates of the impact of each belief of the credibility the mass of our beliefs in this domain. Instead, we use summary rules of varying generality. These rules are quite different from the rules of chess, however. They are not simply chosen at will but mirror, in a systematic and manageable form, our confidence in particular beliefs, classes of beliefs, and combinations of beliefs. Theoretically, there is no control (except perhaps that of the demand for consistency) over the design of games, no external requirements they need meet. The rules we use in general justification of belief are subject to the requirement that they be true to our credibilities on the whole. If a rule conflicts with our credibilities, it will be scrapped. We may say that rules are justified if they adequately reflect our credibilities by selecting those groups of beliefs that rank highest in this regard. A particular belief, then, is justified by its conformity with rules so justified. In effect, it is justified if it hangs together with that family of beliefs that as a whole commands our highest degree of confidence.

Formal logic as a code of valid inference provides an instructive example. People judged good and bad arguments long before the Aristotelian code. The latter was intended to systematize individual judgments and derives its authority from its adequacy as a systematization. When we now refer the justification of a particular inference to the ruling of Aristotle, our procedure depends on our confidence in this adequacy. It is a shorthand way of seeing whether or not the inference belongs with the mass of inferences we find most acceptable. Theoretically, no element in our procedure is free from future reappraisal. If, at some future time, we find that the existing code demands the abandonment of an inference that we value or the acceptance of an inference that we detest, we may alter the code. If an inference we are attached to conflicts with our code, we may give up the inference. There is a mutual adjustment of rules and instances toward selection of that family of instances that, as a whole, has the highest claim on our acceptance. An instance or rule that interferes with such selection is subject to rejection.

Codes of deductive or inductive logic may be construed as definitions of valid inference, not in the sense in which definitions may be used to introduce coined terms, but rather in the sense in which we set about defining a term already in common use, where this use controls our definition. The man who invented Scrabble was defining the game in the first sense by laying down rules that were labeled 'Scrabble Rules.' On the other hand, if a man from Mars were to arrive in the midst of a Scrabble tournament, without benefit of prior study of the official rules, and were asked after some hours to define the game, his task would be considerably different from that of the inventor. He would have to observe, guess, and test, to determine whether his proposed list of defining rules actually squared with the moves of the players. He would be attempting a definition in the second sense.

Even this task would be simpler than that of defining valid inference or, indeed, of defining any term in general use. For our man from Mars could always, as a final resort, check his definition against the official rule book. But for valid inference as for other notions in general use there is no official rule book at all. We start by proposing a definition that will serve as a simplified guide to usage but continue to check our proposal against actual use. We justify a particular use of a term by appeal, not just to any definition, but to one that we feel is itself justified by adequate codification of usage. In effect, we justify a particular use by checking it, through adequate definitions, against all our other uses.

These examples illustrate what we may expect and what we may hope to accomplish in the general justification of moves. Justification in relation to a given set of rules is useless unless the latter are themselves justified. But further relative justification by reference to other sets of rules is fruitless. Somewhere there must be control of rule-sets by initial commitments to moves themselves. The rules we appeal to in justifying social moves are rules that we hope are themselves adequate codifications of our initial commitments. The rules we appeal to select those families of moves that, as wholes, command our acceptance to the highest degree. Without initial commitments there can be no general justification, any more than there can be real or controlled definition without initial usage. But the fact that we are attached to a particular move does not mean that we cannot check it against all others we are committed to (by way of rules), any more than our attachment to a particular locution means that we cannot check it against others we hold proper (by way of controlled definitions). Our legal and moral rules serve, indeed, to guide the making of particular moves, but their guidance depends on their presumed adequacy in codifying our initial commitments to moves, on the whole.

In accordance with the two senses of justification just discussed, we may distinguish two levels of justification of educational decisions. On one level, justification involves conformity with a set of rules, reference to which may be implicitly understood. Here the issue is relative. We ask, 'Is such-and-such decision justified according to rule-set *S*?' For many purposes, the question is legitimate and important, but the answer is often far from simple, even when the rules are fairly well defined. Relative justification is often a highly complicated, intellectually engaging business. To appreciate this fact, one need only recall that there is a whole profession (law) devoted to solving just such questions as the conformity of cases to rule. In education, such justification seems to relate not to specific laws but to broad social practices and traditions, the formulation of which has to be abstracted from our history and is itself a difficult job. Still, such traditions are often cited and used as a lever for changing laws as well as individual decisions.

Yet, legitimate as relative questions are, they do not exhaust our queries in educational contexts. We are not always interested merely in knowing that an educational move conforms to some code. We want to press the issue of deciding among codes. We ask that our moves be justified in terms of some justified code. If our previous analysis is correct, we are seeking justification by rules themselves controlled by the mass of our initial commitments. Of the two levels of justification in educational contexts, the relative type is familiar. The practical issues here may be complicated, and one factor often adds to the complexity: ostensible questions of relative conformity to a given rule may be decided, partly at least, on independent moral grounds. Yet, many of these issues seem familiar in outline. The understanding of general justification presents a more formidable task, since the formulation of relevant rules is of the difficult variety illustrated by the attempt of the man from Mars to codify the rules of a game by watching the play. We need to do something of this sort, but far more complex, since the activity involved is our own and touches on our fundamental commitments.

What rules do we appeal to in general justification of educational decisions on content? The answer to this question consists of a set of rules, not assertions, but the process of compiling an adequate set of rules is as empirical a task as can be imagined. Definitions are not assertions; but to compile a set of definitions one needs to call on all sorts of information, hypotheses, hunches —and the resulting set is always subject to recall, if not to falsification. It is with such qualifications that I offer my list of rules relating to decisions on curriculum. This list should be construed as a hypothesis, tentatively offered and inviting criticism. If it proves wrong, the process of correcting it will itself help clarify the grounds of our curricular decisions.

To simplify our considerations, let us avoid, at least at the outset, the problem of formulating special, complicated rules for deciding on content to be taught at a particular time and in particular circumstances. Let us consider instead all the content to be learned by a child during his formal schooling. Without worrying, for the moment, about the functions of particular segments of this content, let us ask instead what we expect of the content as a whole. Let us, further, state our rules in terms broad enough to allow for practical judgment in applying them to cases.

The guiding principle underlying the following rules is that educational content is to help the learner attain maximum self-sufficiency as economically as possible.

Presumably, self-sufficiency can be brought about economically or extravagantly; content should be selected that is judged most economical. Three types of economy are relevant. First, content should be economical of teaching effort and resources. Second, content should be economical of learners' effort. If a very strenuous way and a very easy way of learning something are otherwise equal, this rule would have us select the easier course. Some such principle seems to figure often in educational discussion. For example, the linking of subject matter to children's interests is often defended on grounds that this technique facilitates learning, and even opponents of this approach do not argue that these grounds are irrelevant. It is important, however, to specify that our rules all contain a tacit clause: 'other things being equal.' It may be argued, for example, that the strenuous course makes for perseverance and other desirable habits, as the easy course does not. Here, however, other things are not equal, and the present rule fails to apply. Criticism of extremism in progressive education, for instance, may be interpreted as insisting that the 'interest' principle never stands alone but is always qualified by the clause 'other things being equal.' Once qualified, the rule stands, in my opinion. There is no positive virtue in unnecessarily taxing the learner; his energy may better be saved for other tasks.

Finally, we must consider economy of subject matter; content should have maximum generalizability or transfer value. The notion of generalizability is, however, ambiguous. Accordingly, two types of subject-matter economy need to be distinguished. First, is there an empirically ascertainable tendency for the learning of some content to facilitate other learning? Presumably, this sort of question was at issue in the controversy over classics, and it was discussed in terms of empirical studies. Second, is the content sufficiently central logically to apply to a wide range of problems? This is not a psychological question but one that concerns the structure of available knowledge. Nevertheless, it is through some such principle of economy, in the logical sense, that we decide to teach physics rather than meteorology, for instance, where other considerations are balanced.

The most economical of contents in all the aspects described must still meet the requirements of facilitating maximum self-sufficiency. It should be obvious that we do not necessarily, or ever, apply first the rules of economy and then the rules of self-sufficiency. These rules represent, rather, various requirements put on content, and we may apply them in various orders or simultaneously. We turn now to the rules of self-sufficiency.

Content should enable the learner to make responsible personal and moral decisions. Self-awareness, imaginative weighing of alternative courses of action, understanding of other people's choices and ways of life, decisiveness without rigidity, emancipation from stereotyped ways of thinking and perceiving—all these are bound up with the goal of personal and moral self-sufficiency. The problem of relating school subjects to such traits is an empirical one, but I think it extremely unlikely that a solution is to be found in the mechanical correlation of each subject to some one desired trait. Rather, the individual potentialities of each subject are likely to embrace many desired habits of mind. The use of literature to develop empathy is often noted. But to suppose that this function is restricted to literature is to impoverish our view of the potentialities of other subjects. Anthropology, history, and the other human sciences also offer opportunities to empathize. But even the natural sciences and mathematics may be seen not merely as technical equipment but as rich fields for the exercise of imagination, intuition, criticism, and independent judgment.

The making of responsible personal and moral decisions requires certain traits of character and habits of mind, but such decision-making also requires reliable knowledge, embodied in several areas of study. Psychology, anthropology, and other human studies illumine personal choice; history, political science, economics, sociology and related areas illumine the social background of choices of career and ideology.

We have spoken of personal and moral self-sufficiency, but this is not enough. Since personal and moral decisions are not made in a vacuum, their execution requires technical skills of various sorts. Content should thus provide students with the technical or instrumental prerequisites for carrying out their decisions. What this goal may require in practice will vary from situation to situation; but, speaking generally, mathematics, languages, and the sciences are, I believe, indispensable subjects, while critical ability, personal security, and independent power of judgment in the light of evidence are traits of instrumental value in the pursuit of any ends. In creating curriculums, the notion of technical or instrumental self-sufficiency provides a counterbalance to emphases on the child's interest. For subjects unsupported by student interest may yet have high instrumental value for the students themselves. To avoid teaching them such subjects is, in the long run, to hamper their own future self-sufficiency, no matter what their future aims may be. Thus, it is misleading to label as an imposition of adult values the teaching of instrumentally valuable subjects.

Finally, beyond the power to make and to carry out decisions, self-sufficiency requires intellectual power. Content, that is, should provide theoretical sophistication to whatever degree possible. Here we may distinguish between logical, linguistic, and critical proficiency—the ability to formulate and appraise arguments in various domains, on the one hand, and acquaintance with basic information as well as with different modes of experience and perception, on the other. The danger here, a serious risk of general education programs, is that of superficiality. But ignorance is also a danger. How to avoid both ignorance and superficiality is the basic practical problem. I should hazard the opinion that the solution lies not in rapid survey courses but in the intensive cultivation of a small but significant variety of areas.

10

Reflections on educational relevance

J. L. Austin used to query the importance of importance. I want here to question the educational relevance of educational relevance.

To do so may seem paradoxical, even absurd. For if relevance is not relevant, what is? And who, in his right mind, would wish learning to be irrelevant? The air of obviousness about these questions misleads, however. It derives, not from some mythical relevance axiom of the theory of education, but from the characteristic value-laden import of the word in its categorical use. To stand against irrelevance is like opposing sin and to favor relevance is akin to applauding virtue. The theoretical problem, with relevance as with virtue, is to say in what it consists and why, thus specified, it ought to be pursued. Relevance is, in particular, not an absolute property; nothing is either relevant or irrelevant in and of itself. Relevant to what, how, and why?—that is the question. That is, at any rate, the question if the current demand for relevance is to be taken not merely as a fashionable slogan but as a serious educational doctrine.

There being no single official elaboration of such a doctrine, I shall sketch three philosophical interpretations that might plausibly be offered in defense of current emphases on relevance, and I shall organize my comments around each of these interpretations. The first is primarily epistemological, concerning the nature and warrant of knowledge. The second is primarily psychological, having to do with the character of thought. The third is mainly moral, treating of the purposes of schooling.

Epistemological interpretation

According to a venerable tradition, knowing is a state of union

First given as a lecture in a series on 'University Problems' at Brandeis University, Fall, 1969. Subsequently presented at a symposium on the 'Concept of Relevance in Education,' sponsored by the American Philosophical Association, Eastern Division, December 1969. Published in *Journal of Philosophy*, Vol. LXVI (1969), 764-73; reprinted by permission of the publisher.

of the knower and the known. In apprehension, the knower is at one with the object, contemplation a form of love in which rational man finds his highest consummation. The state of union is of course not physical; to know a thing is not to be in physical proximity to it. Rather, it is to understand it, that is, to apprehend through the mind its essential structure or abstract form. Knowledge is union, then, not with the ordinary things of the world, but with their ideal essences. Such union affords, however, an indirect grasp of ordinary things and processes, inasmuch as the latter are crude approximations or rough embodiments of the pure forms seen by the eye of intellect alone.

For the Platonic tradition just sketched, knowing thus involves a withdrawal from the immediate world as well as an identification of the mind with the abstract forms which alone render this world intelligible. Education is not an immersion in the ordinary world but an approach to a superior abstract reality remote from it. Ideally, education is mathematical and dialectical, and the mind illuminated by abstract forms is best able to deal with the ordinary processes of the physical and human environment when it is once again directed toward them.

The classical conception we have been discussing has been largely abandoned. The doctrine of abstract forms, in particular, has been severely criticized. There are, to begin with, fundamental difficulties in conceiving the nature and interrelations of these forms, as well as their relations to the ordinary world. The rise of scientific modes of thought has, moreover, made it increasingly implausible to suppose that knowledge consists in contemplation of a world of essences, of superior reality, lying behind the changing phenomena of the common-sense environment. The world of changes is the one real world. Through addressing itself actively to this world, science seeks the provisional experimental truths that dwell amid change.

From this point of view, an education that draws the student away from the phenomena of his environment diverts him from the task of achieving truth. If the notion of a static world of essences is rejected as myth, an education that encourages the mind to dwell in such a world must frustrate the pursuit of truth. Detached and abstract, it is irrelevant to the only reliable processes available to man for establishing true beliefs by which he can guide his conduct. Such epistemological irrelevance is to be shunned if rational conduct is our ideal. Instead of withdrawal, education must encourage immersion in the changing phenomena constituting the live environment of the student. The radical rejection of classical doctrines of knowledge thus leads us to reject equally a detached and remote education.

Now the trouble with this line of thought, as I see it, is not that it rejects classical epistemology, but that it does not sufficiently reject it. Denying the Platonistic assumption of a superior world of essences, it retains the ancient and even more primitive assumption that knowledge consists in a state of union between knower and known. To know is to draw near to, and be one with, the object of knowledge, to eliminate the distance between. Instead of the object of knowledge being thought to consist in an essential and superior reality, it is now conceived simply as the ordinary world of material and historical processes. To know this object is, however, again to be understood as consisting in a state of union with it. This ordinary world must be directly confronted, without conventional or ideological intermediaries. Education is to abolish distance and detachment, bringing the learner into intimate engagement with the environment to be known.

The underlying assumption of knowledge as union is, however, radically false. Glued to the phenomena, the mind can no more attain perspective than can the viewer with eyeballs glued to the painting. Cognition is inextricably dependent upon categorization, analysis, selection, abstraction, and expectation. It is the very antithesis of dumb contract. If the scientist does not seek to contemplate a static world of essences, neither does he immerse himself in the phenomenal changes of his immediate environment in an effort to confront the facts. Facts, in any case, presuppose conceptualization and derive significance through their bearings on theory. The scientist, far from rejecting the mediation of concepts and theoretical construction, seeks ever newer and more comprehensive intellectual schemes for understanding. These schemes bring with them fresh modes of analysis and order; they create novel definitions of fact and bring forth new dimensions of relevance. What the scientist rejects is the rule of the familiar. His job is precisely not to take for granted the customary conceptual apparatus of his environment but, through criticism and invention, to develop more adequate intellectual equipment which will encompass this very environment along with other actual and possible ones.

Such a mission requires that he step back from the material and conceptual surroundings in which he finds himself. He seeks the distance that lends perspective and the critical detachment that facilitates alternative testable visions. There is a world of difference between such withdrawal and the retreat into never-never lands of myth or pedantry. The alternative to such retreat is not a warm bath in immediate phenomena but a search for theoretical comprehension that transcends the merely local and the merely customary. Epistemological relevance, in short, requires us to reject both myth and mystic union. It requires not contact but criticism, not immersion in the phenomenal and conceptual given, but the flexibility of mind capable of transcending, reordering, and expanding the given. An education that fosters criticism and conceptual flexibility will transcend its environment not by erecting a mythical substitute for this world but rather by striving for a systematic and penetrating comprehension of it.

Psychological interpretation

Thought, according to a widely prevalent doctrine, is problem-oriented. It originates in doubt, conflict, and difficulty. Its function is to overcome obstacles to the smooth flow of human activities. When action is coherent and well adapted to its circumstances, human energy is released into overt channels set by habit and custom. The blocking of conduct, either through internal conflict or environmental hindrance, turns its energy inwards, transforming it into thought. Playing out multiple possibilities for future action, thought proceeds until an envisaged feature of some such possibility sparks overt conduct once more, conduct which, by its impact on surrounding conditions, may succeed in overcoming the initial hindrance to the regular outward flow of action. In the evolutionary perspective, thought is an adaptive instrument for overcoming environmental difficulties. Scientific inquiry, the most highly developed form of thought, is the most effective reaction to such difficulties, and the most explicitly problem-directed.

In general, we may say that when thought is genuine and effective it is a response to an objective breakdown in the organization of habit and belief, an answer to the torment of doubt. Controlled by its initiating perplexity, its effectiveness may be gauged by the extent to which it achieves resolution of the difficulty that gave it birth. Thought that is not thus relevant to a problem does not constitute genuine inquiry or deliberation. An education geared to the encouragement of the latter must, then, take its starting point in the doubts and difficulties of the student, originating in his life conflicts and the social issues of his environment. Its relevance to live problems must be evident in its ultimate motivation, which is to solve these problems, and in its evaluation as facilitating or retarding such solutions.

Now it is easy to read this pragmatic doctrine of thought as a merely descriptive account, but such a reading would be mistaken. The doctrine is not designed to embrace all activity that might readily be described as thinking in everyday parlance. In musing, recollecting, or imagining, one is thinking though not necessarily solving problems. The work of painter, writer, or composer, thoughtful and focused as it is, cannot readily be taken as a species of problem solving: of what problem is *Macbeth* the solution? The artist's activity does not always originate in the breakdown of habit, nor is it plausibly split into internal deliberation and overt unthinking action, rather than taken as a continuous flow in which making and thinking are smoothly meshed. In attending to my words now, you are thinking, but you have not, I hope, experienced an objective breakdown at the outset of my paper.

The fundamental import of the pragmatic doctrine is, I suggest, rather normative than descriptive. It purports to tell us what *genuine* thinking consists in. Taking its cue from evolutionary categories, it stresses the adaptive function of thinking in the organism's struggle to survive in a hostile or indifferent environment. Interpreting science as the most refined and effective development of such adaptive thinking, it urges the ostensible problem-solving pattern of scientific research as the chief paradigm of intellectual activity, to be favored in all phases of education and culture.

To say that the problem theory of thinking is normative in its import does not, however, imply that it rests on no factual assumptions whatever. As we have just noted, it draws particularly upon a special reading of science as the prime example of responsible and effective thinking, growing out of practical problems and issuing in reconstructed modes of conduct. And this reading cannot, I believe, be sustained. It holds at best for simple types of practical thinking and for technological applications, but it does no justice to science as an autonomous theoretical endeavor. Scientific theories do not, generally, grow out of practical conflicts, nor do they, in themselves, serve to guide practical activities; they are embedded in complex intellectual structures linked only indirectly, and as wholes, to contexts of evidence and experiment. Their assessment is intimately dependent upon these intellectual structures, and involves, aside from practical efficacy, theoretical considerations bearing on their relative simplicity, naturalness, comprehensiveness, elegance, and connectibility with associated structures.

The scientist's work may perhaps be plausibly described as problem-oriented, in that much of it is directed toward the answering of certain questions. But these questions cannot be identified with practical breakdowns in the personal life or social environment of the scientist. They typically cannot even be understood outside the historical context of prior theorizing and experimentation, which determines independent canons of intellectual relevance. The scientist's questioning is, moreover, often hypothetical and speculative. Born of a sophisticated curiosity, it may come to torment his waking hours; it does not itself need to originate in personal or social torment. Even Charles Sanders Peirce, the father of pragmatism, who began by insisting on real and active doubt as the first phase of thought, had increasingly to emphasize the significance of feigned doubt in order to account for the autonomous context of scientific problem solving. An educational conception of thinking as directly addressed to the alleviation of conflicts and breakdowns of behavior would, in sum, constitute not the foundation of a scientific attitude of mind but the death knell of scientific thought. By confining thought to the immediacies of practice, it would eliminate its leverage on practice, reducing its characteristic effectiveness in transforming the environment.

Nor does the problem theory of inquiry, even broadly interpreted in terms of questions, tell the whole story. Thought does not subside when doubts are, for the moment, stilled. A scientist without questions is not a happy, thoughtless theorist. Problem finding is at least as important to him as problem solving. He does not, in any event, wait upon difficulties that happen to occur to him, but strenuously seeks new difficulties of the widest critical significance. An education modeled on scientific thinking could not possibly remain content with the student's initial problems; it would seek to introduce him to new ones and train him to explore further for himself. More generally, it would strive to create wider perception as well as to improve problem-solving capacity, to develop an alertness to unsettled and conflicting elements in experience as well as a drive to organize, unify, and resolve. It would, in short, aim not only to assess ideas by their relevance to given questions, but also to discover new questions by expanding the sense of relevance.

Moral interpretation

If a defense of educational relevance is to be found neither in the notion of knowledge as union nor in the conception of thought as a response to practical difficulty, can we not hope to find such a defense by considering the purposes of schooling? Granted that knowledge presupposes critical perspective and that the life of thought has its own integrity, is there no practical value to be gained by the development of theoretical understanding? Do we not need to make special provision for bringing such understanding to earth, for applying it toward the resolution of the practical problems of men? Indeed, considering the institution of schools, is it not clear that their primary purpose is to foster the employment of knowledge for desirable social ends?

Reflections such as these, by offering a more restricted interpretation of relevance than the preceding two we have considered, seem to gain in persuasiveness. Social relevance is not to be construed as a necessary feature of all knowledge or thought. Rather, it is a consequence of the primary institutional function of the school. The school's job, after all, is not confined to the advancement of knowledge and the fostering of scientific habits of mind. For knowledge and critical thought are themselves valued for their potential contribution to the achievement of social goals. Such contribution requires not merely the advancement but the employment of knowledge; it depends upon developing not only habits of inquiry but also arts of application. Indeed, application is the ultimate end to which inquiry is a means, and, from the standpoint of society, the school must thus be viewed as an instrument for the realization of its goals. The relation between knowledge and application is, furthermore, not an internal or necessary one; without special care, knowledge may very well be pursued without thought of its practical use. All the more reason, then, to build the context of social application into the life of the school as an encompassing emphasis in relation to which training in inquiry may be seen in its proper instrumental light.

Seen in long-term perspective, then, the school is a means for the improvement of society. The ultimate fruit of the knowledge it seeks is its use in life. Schooling must thus be so organized as to bring knowledge to bear on life's problems and, in so doing, to train students in the proper application of what they may know or come to know. Practical problems of the larger community should serve to provide the major framework within which all the school's activities are set. Separate as abstract intellectual specialties, the school's subjects are to be brought together in their common application to shared social problems. Curricular integration is to be accomplished not by some internal structural scheme but by a pervasive view of the content of schooling as an instrument in the service of the larger society. Education is thus to be made relevant by making its instrumental values dominant. A remote education, bringing nothing to the resolution of the problems of society, is a luxury society neither can nor should allow.

There is much in the foregoing interpretation that seems to me compelling. To argue, as I did earlier, that thought is not generally to be conceived as a response to practical difficulty and that theoretical inquiry involves critical distance and autonomous development does not, after all, imply that practical application is to be shunned. There is no warrant for the stark doctrine that schooling is practical only if thought itself is a practical tool, that, conversely, if thought is independent of practice then schooling must itself be divorced from the life of the surrounding community. The root assumption that the scope of schooling is fixed by the limits of thought must itself be rejected as the source of much mischief.

Theoretical inquiry, independently pursued, has the most powerful potential for the analysis and transformation of practice. The bearing of inquiry upon practice is, moreover, of the greatest educational interest. Such interest is not, contrary to recent emphases, exhausted in a concern for inquiry within the structures of the several disciplines. Students should be encouraged to employ the information and techniques of the disciplines in analysis, criticism, and alteration of their practical outlooks. Habits of practical diagnosis, critique, and execution based upon responsible inquiry need to supplement theoretical attitudes and disciplinary proficiencies in the training of the young. In so far as the doctrine of educational relevance is to be taken as emphasizing this point, I find myself in complete agreement with it. The example of professional education here points the way. Medical education, for example, must embrace not only disciplinary inquiries but also the arts of judgment and application to cases. And what holds for the specialized concerns of the professions seems to me to hold for schooling generally as an institution of society.

Yet reference to professional education suggests also certain respects in which the interpretation we have been considering is overdrawn. To insist that application is essential to professional training does not imply that it must dominate; to acknowledge the contribution of theoretical inquiry in transforming practice is not to argue that theory is to be treated as solely instrumental. Theory is effective in so far as it provides insight into fundamental processes, and the quest for such insight cannot be systematically bent to any external requirement without hampering its development and its consequent effectiveness. Professional education needs to bring the concerns of independent inquiry and the challenge of a specific range of practical problems into communication; it needs to foster mutual respect and understanding between researchers and practitioners. It cannot require research to be pursued in a practical frame of mind nor impose a uniform instrumental framework upon its constituent activities without reducing its own efficacy.

The conclusion is even stronger when we consider not professional education, oriented as it is toward special social functions, but schooling generally. For the potential ramifications of knowledge cannot be determined in advance; to encase all schooling within the framework of specified applications to practice is to hinder severely its unknown developments in other directions as well as its capacity to generate alternative conceptions of application.

Indeed, the notion that education is an instrument for the realization of social goals, no matter how worthy they are thought to be, harbors the greatest conceivable danger to the ideal of a free and rational society. For if these goals are presumed to be fixed in advance, the instrumental doctrine of schooling exempts them from the critical scrutiny that schooling itself may foster. On the other hand, if these goals are themselves to be subject to public criticism and review, schools may be conceived as social instruments only in the broad sense in which they also facilitate independent evaluation of social practice, only if they are, in effect, conceived as instruments of insight and criticism, standing apart from current social conceptions and serving autonomous ideals of inquiry and truth. A society that supports this conception of schooling is one which, rather than setting external limits to its work, is prepared to incorporate the school's loyalties to independent inquiry and free criticism into its own basic structure and ideals. In effect, such a society must view itself as instrumental to the values of schooling quite as much as it takes schools to serve its own goals.

A conception such as this is indeed what one would expect from an instrumentalism inspired by Dewey's notion of the continuity between means and ends, and it is ironic that the main stress in certain passages of his work is on the school as means. When one considers, however, that Dewey takes the end to be not society as it happens to be, but a reformed society, illuminated by an ideal imagination and a critical intelligence that it is the school's office to foster, it becomes clear that any simple-minded doctrine of the school as social instrument is inadequate, both as an expression of Dewey's views and as an independently persuasive educational philosophy. For the fact is that the larger society that the school is said to serve at any given time cannot be taken for granted as providing an ultimate end. It must itself be judged worthwhile by reference to the rational standards and the heritage of critical values to which the school bears witness. If the fruit of knowledge is its use in life, it must be a life itself infused with a respect for knowledge and criticism. It is, in short, one thing to say that the content of schooling should be brought to bear upon practice, that free inquiry and practical concerns are to be put into communication. It is quite another to say that schooling is to be conceived as an instrument for the implementation of designated social values, taken as ultimate.

This point of difference is decisive. To make education relevant by making it instrumental in the latter sense is to destroy its autonomy and to deliver it to the rule of uncriticized social values. To recognize, on the other hand, that the responsibility of education is not only to serve but also to criticize, enlighten, and create—that its job is not only to provide persons with techniques but, more importantly, to provide techniques with critical, informed, and humane persons—is to realize that it has its own dignity and its own direction to follow. Its primary task is not to be relevant but to help form a society in which its ideals of free inquiry and rationality shall themselves have become chief touchstones of relevance.

Moral education and the democratic ideal

Introduction

What should be the purpose and content of an educational system in a democratic society, in so far as it relates to moral concerns? This is a very large question, with many and diverse ramifications. Only its broadest aspects can here be treated, but a broad treatment, though it must ignore detail, may still be useful in orienting our thought and highlighting fundamental distinctions and priorities.

Education in a democracy

Commitment to the ideal of democracy as an organizing principle of society has radical and far-reaching consequences, not only for basic political and legal institutions, but also for the educational conceptions that guide the development of our children. All institutions, indeed, operate through the instrumentality of persons; social arrangements are 'mechanisms' only in a misleading metaphorical sense. In so far as education is considered broadly, as embracing all those processes through which a society's persons are developed, it is thus of fundamental import for all the institutions of society, without exception. A society

Originally prepared at the invitation of Representative John Brademas, Chairman, Select Subcommittee on Education, Committee on Education and Labor of the House of Representatives. It was offered as a background paper for the Subcommittee's hearings on the proposed National Institute of Education. A version also appears in *Educational Research: Prospects and Priorities*, Appendix 1 to Hearings on H.R. 3606, Committee Print, 92nd Congress, 2nd Session, Washington: US Government Printing Office, 1972. Written in response to a growing interest in moral education as a special area or aspect of schooling, the paper stresses the connections between moral, scientific, and democratic education and the centrality, in all three, of the habits of critical thought. (Extracts from R. B. Perry, *Realms of Value*, 1954, by permission of Harvard University Press.)

committed to the democratic ideal is one that makes peculiarly difficult and challenging demands of its members; it accordingly also makes stringent demands of those processes through which its members are educated.

What is the democratic ideal, then, as a principle of social organization? It aims so to structure the arrangements of society as to rest them ultimately upon the freely given consent of its members. Such an aim requires the institutionalization of reasoned procedures for the critical and public review of policy; it demands that judgments of policy be viewed not as the fixed privilege of any class or élite but as the common task of all, and it requires the supplanting of arbitrary and violent alteration of policy with institutionally channeled change ordered by reasoned persuasion and informed consent.

The democratic ideal is that of an open and dynamic society: open, in that there is no antecedent social blueprint which is itself to be taken as a dogma immune to critical evaluation in the public forum; dynamic, in that its fundamental institutions are not designed to arrest change but to order and channel it by exposing it to public scrutiny and resting it ultimately upon the choices of its members. The democratic ideal is antithetical to the notion of a fixed class of rulers, with privileges resting upon social myths which it is forbidden to question. It envisions rather a society that sustains itself not by the indoctrination of myth, but by the reasoned choices of its citizens, who continue to favor it in the light of a critical scrutiny both of it and its alternatives. Choice of the democratic ideal rests upon the hope that this ideal will be sustained and strengthened by critical and responsible inquiry into the truth about social matters. The democratic faith consists not in a dogma, but in a reasonable trust that unfettered inquiry and free choice will themselves be chosen, and chosen again, by free and informed men.

The demands made upon education in accord with the democratic ideal are stringent indeed; yet these demands are not ancillary but essential to it. As Ralph Barton Perry has said: [1]

Education is not merely a boon conferred by democracy, but a condition of its survival and of its becoming that which it undertakes to be. Democracy is that form of social organization which most depends on personal character and moral autonomy. The members of a democratic society cannot be the wards of their betters; for there is no class of betters ... Democracy demands of every man what in other forms of social organization is demanded only of a segment of society ...

Democratic education is therefore a peculiarly ambitious education. It does not educate men for prescribed places in life, shaping them to fit the requirements of a preexisting and rigid division of labor. Its idea is that the social system itself, which determines what places there are to fill, shall be created by the men who fill them. It is true that in order to live and to live effectively men must be adapted to their social environment, but only in order that they may in the long run adapt that environment to themselves. Men are not building materials to be fitted to a preestablished order, but are themselves the architects of order. They are not forced into Procrustean beds, but themselves design the beds in which they lie. Such figures of speech symbolize the underlying moral goal of democracy as a society in which the social whole justifies itself to its personal members.

To see how radical such a vision is in human history, we have only to reflect how differently education has been conceived. In traditional authoritarian societies education has typically been thought to be a process of perpetuating the received lore, considered to embody the central doctrines upon which human arrangements were based. These doctrines were to be inculcated through education; they were not to be questioned. Since, however, a division between the rulers and the ruled was fundamental in such societies, the education of governing élites was sharply differentiated from the training and opinion-formation reserved for the masses. Plato's *Republic*, the chief work of educational philosophy in our ancient literature, outlines an education for the rulers in a hierarchical utopia in which the rest of the members are to be deliberately nourished on myths. And an authoritative contemporary Soviet textbook on *Pedagogy* declares that, 'Education in the USSR is a weapon for strengthening the Soviet state and the building of a classless society ... the work of the school is carried on by specially trained people who are guided by the state.'[2] The school was indeed defined by the party program of March 1919 as 'an instrument of the class struggle. It was not only to teach the general principles of communism but "to transmit the spiritual, organizational, and educative influence of the proletariat to the half- and nonproletarian strata of the working masses." '[3] In nondemocratic societies, education is two-faced: it is a weapon or an instrument for shaping the minds of the ruled in accord with the favored and dogmatic myth of the rulers; it is, however, for the latter, an induction into the prerogatives and arts of rule, including the arts of manipulating the opinions of the masses.

To choose the democratic ideal for society is wholly to reject the conception of education as an *instrument* of rule; it is to surrender the idea of shaping or molding the mind of the pupil. The function of education in a democracy is rather to liberate the mind, strengthen its critical powers, inform it with knowledge and the capacity for independent inquiry, engage its human sympathies, and illuminate its moral and practical choices. This function is, further, not to be limited to any given subclass of members, but to be extended, in so far as possible, to all citizens, since all are called upon to take part in processes of debate, criticism, choice, and co-operative effort upon which the common social structure depends. 'A democracy which educates for democracy is bound to regard all of its members as heirs who must so far as possible be qualified to enter into their birthright.'[4]

Implications for schooling

Education, in its broad sense, is more comprehensive than schooling, since it encompasses all those processes through which a society's members are developed. Indeed, all institutions influence the development of persons working within, or affected by, them. Institutions are complex structures of actions and expectations, and to live within their scope is to order one's own actions and expectations in a manner that is modified, directly or subtly, by that fact. Democratic institutions, in particular, requiring as they do the engagement and active concern of all citizens, constitute profoundly educative resources. It is important to note this fact in connection with our theme, for it suggests that formal agencies of schooling do not, and cannot, carry the whole burden of education in a democratic society, in particular moral and character education. All institutions have an educational side, no matter what their primary functions may be. The question of moral education in a democracy must accordingly be raised not only within the scope of the classroom but also within the several realms of institutional conduct. Are political policies and arrangements genuinely open to rational scrutiny and public control? Do the courts and agencies of government operate fairly? What standards of service and integrity are prevalent in public offices? Does the level of political debate meet appropriate requirements of candor and logical argument? Do journalism and the mass media expose facts and alternatives, or appeal to fads and emotionalism? These and many other allied questions pertain to the status of moral education within a democratic society. To take them seriously is to recognize that moral education presents a challenge not only to the schools, but also to every other institution of society.

Yet the issue must certainly be raised specifically in connection with schools and schooling. What is the province of morality in the school, particularly the democratic school? Can morality conceivably be construed as a *subject,* consisting in a set of maxims of conduct, or an account of current mores, or a list of rules derived from some authoritative source? Is the function of moral education rather to ensure conformity to a certain code of behavior regulating the school? Is it, perhaps, to involve pupils in the activities of student organizations or in discussion of 'the problems of democracy'? Or, since morality pertains to the whole of what transpires in school, is the very notion of specific moral schooling altogether misguided?

These questions are very difficult, not only as matters of implementation, but also in theory. For it can hardly be said that there is firm agreement among moralists and educators as to the content and scope of morality. Yet the tradition of moral philosophy reveals a sense of morality as a comprehensive institution over and beyond particular moral codes, which seems to me especially consonant with the democratic ideal, and can, at least in outline, be profitably explored in the context of schooling. What is this sense?

It may perhaps be initially perceived by attention to the language of moral judgment. To say that an action is 'right,' or that some course 'ought' to be followed, is not simply to express one's taste or preference; it is also to make a claim. It is to convey that the judgment is backed by reasons, and it is further to invite discussions of such reasons. It is, finally, to suggest that these reasons will be found compelling when looked at impartially and objectively, that is to say, taking all relevant facts and interests into account and judging the matter as fairly as possible. To make a moral claim is, typically, to rule out the simple expression of feelings, the mere giving of commands, or the mere citation of authorities. It is to commit oneself, at least in principle, to the 'moral point of view,' that is, to the claim that one's recommended course has a point which can be clearly seen if one takes the trouble to survey the situation comprehensively, with impartial and sympathetic consideration of the interests at stake, and with respect for the persons involved in the issue. The details vary in different philosophical accounts, but the broad outlines are generally acknowledged by contemporary moral theorists.[5]

If morality can be thus described, as an institution, then it is clear that we err if we confuse our allegiance to any particular code with our commitment to this institution; we err in mistaking our prevalent code for the *moral point of view* itself. Of course, we typically hold our code to be justifiable from the moral point of view. However, if we are truly committed to the latter, we must allow the possibility that further consideration or new information or emergent human conditions may require revision in our code. The situation is perfectly analogous to the case of science education; we err if we confuse our allegiance to the current corpus of scientific doctrines with our commitment to scientific method. Of course we hold our current science to be justifiable by scientific method, but that very method itself commits us to hold contemporary doctrines fallible and revisable in the light of new arguments or new evidence that the future may bring to light. For scientific doctrines are not held simply as a matter of arbitrary preference; they are held for reasons. To affirm them is to invite all who are competent to survey these reasons and to judge the issues comprehensively and fairly on their merits.

Neither in the case of morality nor in that of science is it possible to convey the underlying *point of view* in the abstract. It would make no sense to say, 'Since our presently held science is likely to be revised for cause in the future, let us just teach scientific method and give up the teaching of content.' The content is important in and of itself, and as a basis for further development in the future. Moreover, one who knew nothing about specific materials of science in the concrete could have no conception of the import of an abstract and second-order scientific method. Nevertheless, it certainly does not follow that the method is of no consequence. On the contrary, to teach current science without any sense of the reasons that underlie it, and of the logical criteria by which it may itself be altered in the future, is to prevent its further intelligent development. Analogously, it makes no sense to say that we ought to teach the moral point of view in the abstract since our given practices are likely to call for change in the future. Given practices are indispensable, not only in organizing present energies, but in making future refinements and revisions possible. Moreover, one who had no concrete awareness of a given tradition of practice, who had no conception of what rule-governed conduct is, could hardly be expected to comprehend what the moral point of view might be, as a second-order vantage point on practice. Nevertheless, it does not follow that the latter vantage point is insignificant. Indeed, it is fundamental in so far as we hold our given practices to be reasonable, that is, justifiable in principle upon fair and comprehensive survey of the facts and interests involved.

There is, then, a strong analogy between the moral and the scientific points of view, and it is no accident that we speak of reasons in both cases. We can be reasonable in matters of practice as well as in matters of theory. We can make a fair assessment of the evidence bearing on a hypothesis of fact, as we can make a fair disposition of interests in conflict. In either case, we are called upon to overcome our initial tendencies to self-assertiveness and partiality by a more fundamental allegiance to standards of reasonable judgment comprehensible to all who are competent to investigate the issues. In forming such an allegiance, we commit ourselves to the theoretical possibility that we may need to revise our current beliefs and practices as a consequence of 'listening to reason.' We reject arbitrariness in principle, and accept the responsibility of critical justification of our current doctrines and rules of conduct.

It is evident, moreover, that there is a close connection between the general concept of *reasonableness*, underlying the moral and the scientific points of view, and the democratic ideal. For the latter demands the institutionalization of 'appeals to reason' in the sphere of social conduct. In requiring that social policy be subject to open and public review, and institutionally revisable in the light of such review, the democratic ideal rejects the rule of dogma and of arbitrary authority as the ultimate arbiter of social conduct. In fundamental allegiance to channels of open debate, public review, rational persuasion and orderly change, a democratic society in effect holds its own current practices open to revision in the future. For it considers these practices to be not self-evident, or guaranteed by some fixed and higher authority, or decidable exclusively by some privileged élite, but subject to rational criticism, that is, purporting to sustain themselves in the process of free exchange of reasons in an attempt to reach a fair and comprehensive judgment.

Here, it seems to me, is the central connection between moral, scientific, and democratic education, and it is this central connection that provides, in my opinion, the basic clue for school practice. For what it suggests is that the fundamental trait to be encouraged is that of reasonableness. To cultivate this trait is to liberate the mind from dogmatic adherence to prevalent ideological fashions, as well as from the dictates of authority. For the rational mind is encouraged to go behind such fashions and dictates and to ask for their justifications, whether the issue be factual or practical. In training our students to reason we train them to be critical. We encourage them to ask questions, to look for evidence, to seek and scrutinize alternatives, to be critical of their own ideas as well as those of others. This educational course precludes taking schooling as an instrument for shaping their minds to a preconceived idea. For if they seek reasons, it is their evaluation of such reasons that will determine what ideas they eventually accept.

Such a direction in schooling is fraught with risk, for it means entrusting our current conceptions to the judgment of our pupils. In exposing these conceptions to their rational evaluation we are inviting them to see for themselves whether our conceptions are adequate, proper, fair. Such a risk is central to scientific education, where we deliberately subject our current theories to the test of continuous evaluation by future generations of our student-scientists. It is central also to our moral code, *in so far as* we ourselves take the moral point of view toward this code. And, finally, it is central to the democratic commitment which holds social policies to be continually open to free and public review. In sum, rationality liberates, but there is no liberty without risk.

Let no one, however, suppose that the liberating of minds is equivalent to freeing them from discipline. *Laissez-faire* is not the opposite of dogma. To be reasonable is a difficult achievement. The habit of reasonableness is not an airy abstract entity that can be skimmed off the concrete body of thought and practice. Consider again the case of science: scientific method can be learned only in and through its corpus of current materials. Reasonableness in science is an aspect or dimension of scientific tradition, and the body of the tradition is indispensable as a base for grasping this dimension. Science needs to be taught in such a way as to bring out this dimension as a consequence, but the consequence cannot be taken neat. Analogously for the art of moral choice: the moral point of view is attained, if at all, by acquiring a tradition of practice, embodied in rules and habits of conduct. Without a preliminary immersion in such a tradition —an appreciation of the import of its rules, obligations, rights, and demands—the concept of choice of actions and rules for oneself can hardly be achieved. Yet the prevalent tradition of practice can itself be taught in such a way as to encourage the ultimate attainment of a superordinate and comprehensive moral point of view.

The challenge of moral education is the challenge to develop critical thought in the sphere of practice and it is continuous with the challenge to develop critical thought in all aspects and phases of schooling. Moral schooling is not, therefore, a thing apart, something to be embodied in a list of maxims, something to be reckoned as simply another subject, or another activity, curricular or extracurricular. It does, indeed, have to pervade the *whole* of the school experience.

Nor is it thereby implied that moral education ought to concern itself solely with the general structure of this experience, or with the effectiveness of the total 'learning environment' in forming the child's habits. The critical questions concern the *quality* of the environment: what is the *nature* of the particular school experience, comprising content as well as structure? Does it liberate the child in the long run, as he grows to adulthood? Does it encourage respect for persons, and for the arguments and reasons offered in personal exchanges? Does it open itself to questioning and discussion? Does it provide the child with fundamental schooling in the traditions of reason, and the arts that are embodied therein? Does it, for example, encourage the development of linguistic and mathematical abilities, the capacity to read a page and follow an argument? Does it provide an exposure to the range of historical experience and the realms of personal and social life embodied in literature, the law, and the social sciences? Does it also provide an exposure to particular domains of scientific work in which the canons of logical reasoning and evidential deliberation may begin to be appreciated? Does it afford opportunity for individual initiative in reflective inquiry and practical projects? Does it provide a stable personal milieu in which the dignity of others and the variation of opinion may be appreciated, but in which a common and overriding love for truth and fairness may begin to be seen as binding oneself and one's fellows in a universal human community?

If the answer is negative, it matters not how effective the environment is in shaping concrete results in conduct. For the point of moral education in a democracy is antithetical to mere shaping. It is rather to liberate.

Notes

1 Ralph Barton Perry, *Realms of Value*, Cambridge: Harvard University Press, 1954, pp. 431-2. Excerpt reprinted in I. Scheffler, ed., *Philosophy and Education*, 2nd ed., Boston: Allyn & Bacon, 1966, pp. 32 ff.

2 Cited in Introduction to George S. Counts and Nucia P. Lodge, eds and translators, *I Want To Be Like Stalin: From the Russian Text on Pedagogy* (by B. P. Yesipov and N. K. Goncharov), New York: John Day, 1947, pp. 14, 18. (The materials cited are from the 3rd ed. of the *Pedagogy*, published in 1946.)
3 Frederic Lilge, 'Lenin and the Politics of Education,' *Slavic Review* (June 1968), Vol. xxvii. No. 2, p. 255.
4 Ralph Barton Perry, *op. cit.*, p. 432.
5 See, for example, Kurt Baier, *The Moral Point of View*, Ithaca: Cornell University Press, 1958; William K. Frankena, *Ethics*, Englewood Cliffs, N.J.: Prentice Hall, 1963, and R. S. Peters, *Ethics and Education*, Glenview, Ill.: Scott Foresman, 1967. Additional articles of interest may be found in Sect. v, 'Moral Education' and Sect. vi, 'Education, Religion, and Politics,' in I. Scheffler, ed., *Philosophy and Education*.

Educational thought

Part 4

Educational liberalism and Dewey's philosophy

12

Though criticism of American education is decidedly no new historical phenomenon, few reflective persons underestimate the severity of the current phase. Nor, while acknowledging its complex roots, do they fail to see its connection with the general regression from liberalism currently in evidence. Within this development, it is not surprising that the educational doctrines of John Dewey, our outstanding recent spokesman of liberalism, should again have become centers of dispute. It is, however, unfortunate that for many concerned with education his work has become an unanalyzable symbol, to be attacked as a whole or defended as a whole, rather than to be studied carefully and evaluated independently. In particular, if we accept Sidney Hook's characterization of Dewey's educational liberalism as involving essentially (a) the application of scientific research and criticism to educational practice, and (b) the application of democratic values and principles to the reform of such practice and its associated institutions and habits of mind, then it seems to me especially unfortunate for proponents of such liberalism to feel that it must always be defended in the context of Dewey's general philosophy. For, aside from considerations of strategy hinging on the fact that such liberalism may validly be supported on widely differing philosophic grounds, I think that certain features of Dewey's general position are independently weak and contribute irrelevant difficulties to the defense of educational liberalism.

In the discussion to follow, I shall try to explain and support this judgment by: (1) briefly sketching Dewey's view of intelligence and learning, (2) discussing some of his dominant emphases in education, and (3) setting forth certain strictures on the foregoing, and related, parts of Dewey's philosophy. For the brevity of my treatment of (1) and (2), I offer only as a minor reason the limitations of space. More important is the fact that

Originally presented as a lecture to the Harvard Hillel Society, May 1956; published in *Harvard Educational Review*, Vol. 26 (1956), 190-8. (Extracts from John Dewey, *Democracy and Education*, copyright 1916 by the Macmillan Company, renewed 1944 by John Dewey.) Reprinted by permission of President and Fellows of Harvard College.

I am here less interested in the meticulous interpretation of Dewey's intentions and the development of his thought than in the objective significance of certain of his recurrent models, metaphors, and key concepts as these have influenced educators.

Dewey's view of intelligence and learning

Dewey's basic modes of thought and argumentation are holistic. A favorite tactic is to interpret the given problem as generated by some philosophic dualism and then to deal with the latter not by adopting one or another of its sides exclusively but rather by showing the partiality of each and the continuity relating both within some inclusive framework. Though such philosophizing is, of course, not new, Dewey's use is distinctive in its close dependence on modern science both for specific findings and as the key model of an evolving framework within which partial and conflicting views grow into unified and organic wholes. His key philosophic terms 'interaction,' 'transaction,' 'situation,' reveal his organic tendency, and his organic view of science is given in his definition, 'Inquiry is the controlled or directed transformation of an indeterminate situation into one that is so determinate in its constituent distinctions and relations as to convert the elements of the original situation into a unified whole.'[1]

Indeed, Dewey's basic philosophic purpose, as revealed in his various writings, may be said to have been the overcoming of inherited and pervasive dualisms between science and morals, theory and practice, mind and body, thought and action, means and ends. To this purpose he develops a special concept of *experience*, reflecting distinctive features of the deliberate *experimentation* of the scientist, quite different from ordinary ideas of experience as just what goes on, or what is passively beheld by someone. Experience, for Dewey, is rather the result of an *interaction* between objective conditions and organic energies, and is educative, as scientific experimentation is ideally, to the extent that it engages the active deliberation, imagination, and motivation of the organism.

To determine the educative potential of experience in any context, Dewey generalizes the features of experimental research as the best accredited source of current knowledge. Such research is not random or routine, but originates in a difficulty, a conflict, an unsettled situation constituting a problem. Hypotheses are generated relative to this problem. Such hypotheses are not final ends but serve as guides for subsequent activity such as observation, data-processing, manipulation, inference; furthermore, these hypotheses are controlled by the outcomes of such activity, i.e., they may turn out warranted and the original problem resolved, or they may prove unwarranted and the original difficulty remain to generate further hypotheses. The settlement of a problematic situation proceeds thus in two phases: *trying*, in which we engage in deliberate activity guided by ideas, and *undergoing*, in which we attend to the consequences of this activity as a control over such ideas. Where these ideas survive the test reliably, they may be taken as embodying an accurate perception of relations between our activity and associated consequences, a perception rendered general and usable in a wide variety of future circumstances by its ideal formulation. It is the growth of such perceptions that renders the environment increasingly meaningful and that, applied toward the control of activity, informs it increasingly with intelligence, and weights it with responsibility. With the increasing responsibility accompanying intelligent control, subjection to blind habit and yielding to whim become avoidable and, indeed, morally wrong for greater and greater areas of our behavior. For the function of intelligence is to *reconstruct* practice by deliberately and imaginatively resolving problems as they occur, i.e., in a way that is more efficient than either stereotyped repetition or random variation in response.

When Dewey's philosophy of experience is put in more directly educational terms, it asserts that all genuine reflection, from the most rudimentary to the most highly abstract, exemplifies a single pattern. It always has its origin in a problem, a blocking of habitual conduct. The energy of outwardly unreleased habits is 'turned inwards' to produce deliberation, a dramatic rehearsal of possible future actions to meet the problem. This 'inner' drama continues until some rehearsed consequence of some possible course sparks 'outward' activity once more, an activity whose reconstruction of conditions may succeed in overcoming the initial block so as to allow once more a smooth flow of behavior. The mind is not passive but active and impulsive throughout the process. Its selectivity helps determine the precise character of the problem; its energy vitalizes the play of ideas, stimulates the rebirth of activity and the consequent reconstruction of conditions. Indeed, there is no longer any sense in speaking of the mind as a separate entity, since no line can be drawn between its functions and the rest of the organism, nor indeed, between it and the environment. Its selectivity is one with the specific nature of the organism, its energy is continuous with the momentum of past habit and with the rechanneled force of new traits and conditions. It is best seen as a certain functioning of the organism, a mode of conduct. There is, then, no split between intelligence and conduct: intelligence is the control of conduct by meaning, i.e., by its perceived consequences, while all conduct is potentially intelligent. The only significant difference that remains is that which separates routine or capricious conduct from conduct intelligently governed by a perception of its meaning. The notion of *technique* is, moreover, not to be identified with blind routine behavior and opposed to intelligence. Technique controlled by meaning is just meaning rendered effective; it is the very opposite of mere routine and is exemplified ideally in the artist. 'The artist is a masterful *technician*. The technique or mechanism is fused with thought and feeling. The mechanical performer permits the mechanism to dictate the performance. It is absurd to say that the latter exhibits habit and the former not. We are confronted with two kinds of habit, intelligent and routine.'[2]

Dewey's dominant emphases in education

Dewey's holism and his emphasis on continuity find explicit application in his treatment of formal education. He opposes strongly any radical division between major branches or types of learning. The usual separation between higher and lower studies, between theoretical and applied sciences, between humanistic and vocational programs he considers an embodiment of the discredited divorce of intelligence from conduct. As rationality is not the exercise of a separate faculty, so enlightenment is not the exclusive result of contact with 'pure' studies capable of engaging such a faculty. Education must, to render intelligence most effective, bring the studies together rather than perpetuate their separateness. It should exhibit technical and vocational studies in their theoretical setting, and should draw attention to their human and social import. Likewise, theoretical and literary studies should be related to the problems of men which they may illuminate, and the technical conditions of their growth or application.

Furthermore, the very division between the school and life outside the school, between learning and living, is one that needs to be overcome. It is based on the idea that the school can, in isolation, provide pure knowledge during a specified interval so as to prepare the student for a lifetime of informed action. But this idea ignores the fact that learning *is* living, that it takes place most effectively, moreover, in live contexts which set real problems and call forth real purposes, that the one significant way to integrate the work of the school is not by mechanical devices but by relating all of it to the life of the wider community.

Finally, Dewey's view stresses not only the continuity among the studies and between the school and life, but also and most fundamentally, the continuity between the specific truth deliberately taught and the wider context of purpose, activity, and social environment in which its meaning becomes manifest to the learner. The teacher must always remember that learning is not passive reception but involves, at its best, active participation governed by perception of meanings in a problematic situation. This means that the whole environment of meanings surrounding the lesson is important as potentially contributing to learning. It means, for example, that the moral atmosphere of the classroom, the encouragement of curiosity and questioning, the relations among students and with the teacher are to be considered, not as irrelevant to the curriculum, but as the very basis of the moral and intellectual learning that goes on in the school whether we deliberately plan it or not. It means, finally, that every item of subject matter to be taught must be provided with context in the learner's perceptions. These perceptions and, indeed, the learner's whole system of motivations must be taken with the utmost seriousness by the teacher. Problems set within this context activate real purposes and interest, challenge genuine effort and discipline important capacities. 'Study is effectual in the degree in which the pupil realizes the place of the ... truth he is dealing with in carrying to fruition activities in which he is concerned. This connection of an object and a topic with the promotion of an activity having a purpose is the first and the last word of a genuine theory of interest in education.'[3]

Two criticisms of Dewey's approach

The power, simplicity, and sensitivity of Dewey's thought on social and educational issues is undeniable. The force of his observations on teaching and learning is immediate, and even where he may be thought wrong in detail, few will deny the suggestiveness of his treatments. As to educational liberalism, there is no doubt that his case for the moral and educational relevance of science and the primacy of critical and democratic values in education is impressive. His way of looking at things together which are commonly held apart, of seeing continuities where others take gaps for granted, must be held a fruitful philosophical approach, justified by its consequences in his own work.

Yet it does have its dangers, and these must be noted despite the persuasive attractiveness of his closely knit system of ideas. To begin with, his very seeing of all things together and, moreover, always in relation to the future condition of man is likely to be too constricting a philosophic stance for many. Dewey's approach, I think, often runs the risk of mistaking valid distinctions for 'divorces,' 'splits,' and 'sharp divisions' to be uniformly washed away, and his overwhelming social and moral concern leads him to underestimate the value of detachment from environing social conditions. Regarding the latter, Bertrand Russell, for example, remarks, 'Dr Dewey's world, it seems to me, is one in which human beings occupy the imagination; the cosmos of astronomy, though of course acknowledged to exist, is at most times ignored.'[4] Both dangers of his approach may be illustrated in connection with two distinctions which Dewey strongly criticizes. These distinctions, it seems to me, are not only aids to clarity, but worth preserving for the educational values to which they draw attention.

(1) Consider Dewey's extended arguments against the 'divorce' of ideas from action, of theory from practice. Presumably the point relates to the analysis of experiment, discussed above, according to which theoretical ideas arise out of disorganized practical situations and guide further activities by whose outcomes they are controlled. Thus the very function of ideas is to transform action and, consequently, the environment. 'Ideas are worthless except as they pass into actions which rearrange and reconstruct in some way, be it little or large, the world in which we live.'[5] Dewey's polemic against divorcing theory from practice may be construed as an attack upon ideas that are worthless in the sense indicated.

Now Dewey's view seems in great part motivated by emphasis on the empirical control over ideas in science, and what he opposes is the irresponsible assertion of claims unwarranted by empirical evidence. But his conception of the nature of empirical control is, it seems to me, unduly narrow, and fails to do justice to abstract, theoretical considerations in the scientific assessment of evidence. Ideas in science are not all of one kind and only certain simple types can be analyzed as instruments for transforming the world. With the growth of complicated theoretical structures, fundamental statements in science can no longer be understood in the same way. They do not refer to our common world, which is describable by empirical evidence, and they do not, in themselves, guide our activities at all. It is only the whole many-leveled structures in which they are embedded which tie up, at sporadic points, with our world of evidence and action. Since they must, moreover, meet such requirements as simplicity, formulation in acceptable terms, naturalness, likelihood of connection with other structures, etc., their superiority over alternatives within given systems is often not a question of systematic superiority in 'passing into actions which reconstruct the world in which we live,' but is judged in purely theoretical terms.

Dewey's emphasis on empirical control is perhaps then best expressed if we take his above statement to refer, not to single theories, but to whole systematic structures themselves. Granting that parts of such structures need not themselves connect up with our world, we may interpret him as insisting that the whole structures must make connection, though purely theoretical considerations indeed enter into their design and acceptance.

Nevertheless, there remains an ambiguity in the notion of 'our world' or, as Dewey puts it, 'the world in which we live.' For though this phrase is indeed often used to refer to the world in which we here, now, and in the foreseeable future live and act, our scientific systems connect up with various segments of a world that is indefinitely wider in scope, a world to which the same phrase may also be construed to refer. To argue, from the way in which scientific systems significantly connect up with this wide world, against ideas that fail to tie up with our limited future world of practice would be clearly fallacious.

If we now leave the realm of scientific logic and ask what *educational* value could possibly reside in such ideas, it seems to me that it is just their transcendence of our own practical environment that enables them to enlarge the intellectual perspectives of the student. What is of questionable educational value is trivial, petty, narrow learning, not theoretical study which, though illuminating broad reaches of our world, is without practical reference for our own present and future problems. If such study is thus, at least partly, the task of the school, then the school *ought* to stand apart from life in a basic sense: not by cultivating pedantry or myth, but by illuminating a wider world than its limited surroundings and by sustaining those habits of mind that fit it for breadth, penetration, and objectivity of vision. It is not, of course, implied that the school ought not therefore to provide specific preparation for life in the practical future of its pupils. But even where subject matter is taught primarily for its future practical value, students will miss something of high importance if they learn it solely *for the sake of* this practical value. It is important even here for the school to maintain its *autonomous* standards of evaluation by cultivating, as far as possible, an independent appreciation of subject matter and a capacity for purely theoretical curiosity and dispassionate vision.

(2) Consider now Dewey's unified approach to reflective thinking and knowledge, his denial in effect that we can validly distinguish between the descriptive and the instrumental functions of thought. In line with this approach, he attacks conceptions of science as providing fixed ideas which reflect 'antecedent existences,' knowledge which 'is a disclosure of reality ... prior to and independent of knowing .'[6] He insists rather on the problem origin of all thinking, on the consequences of reflection within specific situations, on the functioning of knowledge in life.

> The two limits of every unit of thinking are a perplexed, troubled, or confused situation at the beginning and a cleared-up, unified, resolved situation at the close. The first of these situations may be called *pre*-reflective. It sets the problem to be solved; out of it grows the question that reflection has to answer. In the final situation the doubt has been dispelled; the situation is *post*-reflective; there results a direct experience of mastery, satisfaction, enjoyment. Here, then, are the limits within which reflection falls.[7]

From such a conception of thinking stems the educational emphasis on the purposes, needs, and sensitivities of the child as forming the basic context of learning, since setting the problems which may best motivate reflection. From this conception taken together with the opposition to 'fixity' of ideas comes the natural educational proposal to reorganize traditional blocks of subject matter around problems arising out of felt needs and purposes in life contexts. Now it is nonsense (and Dewey recognized it as such) to appeal to children's transient needs and purposes as a criterion of our long-range educational goals and their associated choices of subject content. Hence the emphasis on such needs and purposes is, I think, best taken as *methodological* advice, logically independent from long-range choice of content-goals, and warranted by the assumption that learning is more efficient as it is directed within *problematic situations from the child's standpoint.*

Now, as thus methodologically conceived, such advice has undeniable relevance for much of our formal education. Yet, taken by itself, it seems to me much too narrow, in effect opposing the 'fixity' of ideas only to replace it by a 'fixity' of problems. Even in so far as it bases itself on the model of scientific inquiry, the attack on fixity of ideas, on knowledge as disclosure of independent existence, seems to me obviously absurd in confusing *facts* with *our attempts to ascertain them, truth* with *confirmation at a given time*.[8] Unless science purports to estimate the facts about events and processes prior to, later than, and independent of our knowing, in quite clear and basic senses, it is a puny enterprise indeed; this is independent of the fact that its *estimates* themselves are obviously neither prior to, later than, nor independent of its estimation, nor fixed in the sense of being immune to revision over time.

But what reason do we have for assimilating all reflective thinking to the problem-solving model in general? In ordinary speech, for example, the poet is thinking in the process of composition, the artist in creation, the translator in attempting a translation, and yet none is seeking the answer to a question.[9] Though subsidiary questions need to be answered in the course of each activity, no *answer* or *set of answers* as such brings each activity to a unified and resolved close; only a satisfactory poem, painting, or translation will do. And what is happening when I on certain occasions think long enough to discover that I have been working on a pseudo-problem? If I am right, then though I was genuinely thinking, my thought grew out of no problem at all. Of course, it will be said that though it grew out of no intelligible *question* it was prompted by uneasiness. But such argument reduces the problem-solving approach to triviality. For aside from the difficulty of distinguishing between *intellectual* uneasiness and the discomfort of, e.g., a cold, strongly motivated daydreams and metaphysical constructions will turn out instances of inquiry in the problem-solving, allegedly scientific sense.

Moreover, the emphasis on the initial problematic contexts of the learner, even from a methodological point of view, seems to me to underplay certain important *educational* values. Foremost among these is the creation of new problems for the learner, the introduction of *unsettled* situations where none existed before. No matter how broadly we may conceive the problems supposed to initiate reflective thinking, our educational purpose is to *create wider perception* as well as to *improve thinking* taken as the settlement of problems. We do not approach our educational tasks within the limits of problems alone, but also with standards of relative importance of problems and we use these as guides to create perceptions that are broader than those of the learner; it is here that perhaps the traditional subjects and standards serve most clearly.

Nor is this an unimportant point generally, for liberalism. For as our culture increasingly distracts us, it becomes easier and easier to avoid significant problems rather than to face them head-on, increasingly possible to stifle our momentary perceptions of evils, especially when remote, and concentrate instead on narrow and personal problems. It is, then, well to remember, especially in our theorizing about education for freedom, that such freedom involves broad and alert perception as well as efficient problem-solving, ability to search out disjointed and unfitting elements in experience, as well as the drive to unify, organize, and settle.

Obviously, of course, I do not for one moment impute to Dewey himself either failure in perception or lack of general recognition of its significance in education. No one who has read him can do this. But I *am* suggesting that some of his basic models in philosophy, and his specific conceptions of inquiry and learning are wrong in certain respects, and that the defense of educational liberalism should not be burdened with their defects. In so far as the cultivation of free habits of mind is educationally of the first importance, there is little argument. If I have, nonetheless, misread Dewey in the opinions of some, I hope that the issues raised will be considered on their own merits and will, furthermore, stimulate the kind of detailed and analytic discussion of his work that alone signifies that it is being taken seriously, in place of the ritualistic use of his name in educational dispute.

Notes

1 John Dewey, *Logic: The Theory of Inquiry*, New York: Henry Holt, 1938, p. 104.
2 John Dewey, *Human Nature and Conduct*, New York: Modern Library, 1930, p. 71, italics mine.
3 John Dewey, *Democracy and Education*, New York: Macmillan, 1916, p. 158.
4 Bertrand Russell, *A History of Western Philosophy*, New York: Simon & Shuster, 1945, p. 827.
5 John Dewey, *The Quest for Certainty*, New York: Minton, Balch, 1929, p. 138. Dewey's complete sentence is, 'For then mankind will learn that, intellectually (that is, save for the esthetic enjoyment they afford, which is of course a true value), ideas are worthless except as . . . .'

6 *Ibid.*, p. 44.

7 John Dewey, *How We Think*, Boston: D. C. Heath, 1910, p. 106.

8 Or, as we may also say, *truth* with *certainty*.

9 For a discussion of this point, see G. Ryle's treatment of thinking in 'Thinking,' *Acta Psychologica*, Vol. IX, 1953, pp. 189-96.

D. J. O'Connor's
An Introduction to the Philosophy of Education

Mr O'Connor's short book[1] is intended both as an elementary account of philosophy of education and as an introduction to philosophical thinking for students of education. Its main purpose, however, is to relate the ideas and methods of contemporary philosophical analysis to educational concerns. In concise and clear style, it first discusses the nature of philosophy and then proceeds to treat of the justification of value judgments, the logic of explanation, the status of educational theories, and the relevance of religion to morals—topics considered by the author as representing the main points of contact between education and philosophy. Each of the chapters succeeds in providing not only a lucid introduction to an important set of problems, but also a stimulating example of philosophical analysis at work. The book is thus admirably suited for use as a text in many introductory courses.

Since the topics it treats are, however, so diverse and so general in import, I have limited the following discussion to two aspects of the book: its philosophic approach and its conception of philosophy of education. The approach of the book is analytic in spirit but refreshingly free from factionalism—showing the influence of different schools of contemporary analysis, and carried through with independence of judgment. Nevertheless, a cautious positivism is discernible in a qualified formulation of the verification theory of meaning, a sustained attack on metaphysics without attempt to define 'metaphysics,' a rejection of ethical cognitivism coupled with a recognition of the inadequacies of persuasive theories of ethics, and an assignment of place of honor to scientific as against other paradigms of analysis.

Each of these four components of O'Connor's treatment raises

Published as a review in *Journal of Philosophy*, Vol. LVI (1959), 766-70; reprinted by permission of the publisher. (Extracts from D. J. O'Connor, *An Introduction to the Philosophy of Education*, Philosophical Library Inc., 1957, by permission of the author and publisher.)

questions of a basic kind. First, consider his discussion of meaning, in which he mentions

> the possibility of a very serious and dangerous kind of philosophical mistake, the making of statements or the asking of questions that have the outward appearance of genuine statements or questions but which, on examination, do not satisfy the criterion that their genuine counterparts must satisfy—namely, possessing a possible range of evidence that, *were it obtainable*, would verify the statement or answer the question (p. 34, italics in original text).

O'Connor tempers this otherwise straightforward restatement of the verification theory by telling us that, 'Unfortunately, it is not possible to give any useful general rules that will enable us to proscribe such statements and questions in advance. We have to test each one and pass or fail it on its merits' (p. 35). The question here is whether the 'criterion' above stated does not itself constitute a purported general rule for deciding meaninglessness. If the criterion is valid, O'Connor's qualification is superfluous. If, presumably in the light of well-known difficulties with the criterion, O'Connor is prepared to admit that meaninglessness must be judged in statement-by-statement fashion, can he still retain the general characterization of significance given in the criterion?

Consider, second, O'Connor's criticism of metaphysical statements, described as those that cannot, in principle, be checked by observation (p. 17, n. 1). He illustrates the category by giving some examples, but warns the reader that not all metaphysical statements are as easy to recognize as his paradigms and that the definition of 'metaphysics' is still a 'live and debatable issue' (p. 17). Since the familiar criticisms of the verification theory apply as well to the general description given of metaphysical statements, is anything to be gained by keeping this description alive, even with the caution that it is theoretically subject to question?

Third, consider the position taken by O'Connor in ethical theory. He admits that persuasive and emotive theories are, so far as we presently know, inadequate in that the distinction between causation and justification is not provided for (pp. 68 ff.). On the other hand, he feels that nonintuitionist, cognitive theories are not merely inadequate but refutable by Hume's argument against the deduction of 'ought' from 'is' (p. 58). Hume, however, does not (and cannot) rule out the possibility of an *explanation* of 'ought,' and Hume's point is, accordingly, convincing only on the extra assumption that there is no appropriate explanation or definition of 'ought.' Bare difference of vocabularies is thus no more sufficient to establish the irreducibility of ethical to nonethical discourse than it is to establish the irreducibility of mathematics to logic. Would it not, then, be more judicious to conclude that both ethical cognitivism and emotivism face problems of comparable sorts?

Finally, consider O'Connor's curious discussion of educational theory. After citing as a major discovery of contemporary analysis (attributed to Moore) the principle that 'the meaning of a word is created and controlled by the ways in which it is used' (p. 37), and after distinguishing several uses of the word 'theory' in order to dispel the fallacy of 'one word—one meaning' (p. 75), he concludes that

> the word 'theory' as it is used in educational contexts is
> generally a courtesy title. It is justified only where we are
> applying well-established experimental findings in psychology
> or sociology to the practice of education. And even here we
> should be aware that the conjectural gap between our theories
> and the facts on which they rest is sufficiently wide to make
> our logical consciences uneasy (p. 110).

One may well ask how this conclusion is to be reconciled with the author's earlier discussions. It is at any rate unclear what warrants it, once we reject the imperialistic notion that scientific uses are always primary. Is it just another vestige of classical positivism seemingly rendered acceptable by the addition of sufficient qualification to undercut it completely?

These questions I have raised are not offered as arguments against O'Connor's own developed position. For his book treats the issues in elementary fashion and is not intended as a full statement of the author's opinions. The questions nevertheless do reflect doubt as to whether the book's cautious positivism is a strong enough foundation on which to build.

In focusing on the logical and linguistic analysis of statements regarded as basic to education, O'Connor's book accords with recent lively interest in the development of an analytic philosophy of education. The *scope* of such a philosophy is, however, a matter on which O'Connor seems to me to vacillate. On the one hand, he states that 'philosophy is not in the ordinary sense of the phrase a body of knowledge but rather an activity of criticism or clarification. As such, it can be exercised on any subject matter at all, including our present concern, the problems of educational theory' (p. 4). On the other hand, he speaks of 'the respective *spheres* of philosophy and education' (p. 2, italics mine), and 'the possible points of contact between the two *subjects*' (p. 2, italics mine), defining 'philosophy of education' as 'those problems *of philosophy* that are of direct relevance to educational theory' (pp. 14-15, italics mine), and declaring that

> no part of philosophy can be separated from the rest except merely for convenience. In introducing philosophy to students of education, we have to make a different selection of problems from the one which would interest students of science or of history. But wherever we begin, we shall be led in the end to the same places (p. 139).

The competition between these two conceptions is of the greatest importance for the development of an analytic philosophy of education. If we picture philosophical analysis as a sovereign subject with its own territory bordering on other dominions only at specific points, we shall be tempted to construe the philosophy of education as having primarily ambassadorial functions—to bring greetings from analysis to the neighboring land of education and to arrange congenial tours for foreigners. If, on the contrary, we picture philosophical analysis as a set of precision tools for the maintenance and repair of delicate intellectual machinery, we shall expect philosophy of education to deal with the most intimate mechanisms of discourse on education: its peculiar idioms and metaphors, forms of reasoning, theoretical conflicts and puzzles, distinctions and classifications.

While O'Connor seems to me to vacillate between these two pictures in explicit statements such as those above cited, his practice, on the whole, tends to support the first rather than the second. In choosing such general problems as the nature of value judgments and explanations and, except for his interesting chapter on educational theories, in omitting topics peculiar to education (e.g., curriculum, teaching and learning, moral training, school and community), his emphasis is on bringing the story of recent analysis to the educator rather than on the analytic clarification of educational ideas. In this, his book is likely to suggest to readers a primarily ambassadorial function for the philosophy of education. And this would, I think, be a pity. There is no need to choose between the investigation of traditional *problems* called 'philosophical' and the perfection of basic intellectual *methods* called 'philosophical.' Analogously, there is no reason

D. J. O'Connor's An Introduction to the Philosophy of Education

to choose between relating the contemporary analysis of these traditional problems to education and applying these basic methods directly to educational problems. In particular, an analytic philosophy of education limited to the first task would be drastically and needlessly impoverished. It is the second task, indeed, constantly overshadowed by traditional conceptions of philosophy as a sovereign subject, that deserves our special solicitude.

Note

1 *An Introduction to the Philosophy of Education,* New York: Philosophical Library, 1957.

A note on
behaviorism as
educational theory

I4

There are, perhaps, considerable gains to be expected from the development of so-called teaching machines and programmed instruction (TMPI, for short). There are surely dangers, however, in a behavioristic rationale that is philosophically naïve or logically confused. For this rationale not only guides the technical work of the laboratory but is offered to the public and profession as *educational theory*, with general import for practice, and moreover, the stamp of scientific authority. A consideration of two pieces in the Fall 1961 issue of the *Harvard Educational Review* will, I believe, indicate certain of the defects and dangers involved. I refer to the article by B. F. Skinner and the review by Harlan Lane.[1]

The 'science' rhetoric, especially in the latter piece, seems to me quite misleading. One would never guess, from the recurrent references to 'a science of behavior,' that psychology and the social sciences are riddled with schools, sects, and fundamental controversies, that learning theory itself is fragmented and fails, in the opinion of many, to approach the scientific status of physical theory, nor that the specifically Skinnerian approach has been subjected to more than one radical and negative conceptual critique in recent years.[2]

Nor could one guess, from Mr Lane's review, that there is any problem in arguing from facts to values, since he is quite forthright in pronouncing *his* values, and makes no effort to avoid giving the impression that these values are uniquely 'objective' and 'scientific.' Indeed, at one point, after telling us what we *must* do ('We *must* review the goals of education, specify the desired behaviors, and examine the means of obtaining—not "developing"—these behaviors, in the light of a science of behavior,' p. 471), he declares that 'to do less is *dishonest*.' In the same direct way, he tells us 'a conception of education is *required* that is consistent with our conception of other areas of applied

---

Harvard Educational Review, Vol. 32 (1962), 210-13. (Copyright 1962 by President and Fellows of Harvard College.)

science'; that 'the traditional image of man is a *cartoon* against the backdrop of modern science'; that 'we *need the courage* to draw up specifications for an educated man that are *not* specifications for ourselves and the *willingness to control behavior* to bring that man about' (p. 471, my italics throughout). He never explains how science can yield all these value judgments nor, alternatively, what their extrascientific warrant might be supposed to be.

As against those interested in experimental comparisons of automated instruction with other methods, Lane denies that such 'evaluation research' is necessary: 'Interest in automated instruction ... has the same justifications as the basic endeavor to understand man's condition and to improve it' (p. 475). And as against those willing to permit the educator to evaluate teaching machines selectively in the light of personal philosophy, Lane declares that 'such an outcome would be disastrous for the ultimate efficacy of automated teaching. What is required of the educator, on the contrary, is a re-evaluation of personal philosophy in the light of the *principles of behavior* that underlie... the technological revolution' (p. 472, my italics). Since even Lane apparently agrees that, as a matter of fact, 'no one point of view is held unanimously among psychologists,' he is here clearly referring to *principles of behavior, as he sees them.* The total upshot is remarkable: the educator's not to question why, his but to accept TMPI *in toto* as Lane interprets it. If no *educational* purpose can, in practice, be shown to be advanced, the educator may rest assured that all is for the glory of the ultimate efficacy of automated teaching.

In Lane's view, finally, the concept linking laboratory and education is *control*, and he says, 'to the extent that we sacrifice this control we impair and deflect the learning process' (p. 473). Without the least acknowledgment of the radical differences in context provided by laboratory and classroom, or of the morally crucial variations in the meaning of 'control,' Lane's discussion glides easily and resoundingly from the notion of *experimental control* to that of *educational manipulation*: 'An analysis of behavior under the *controlled conditions of the laboratory* is propaedeutic to the *manipulation of that behavior* in the complex environment of the classroom' (p. 475). It would be hard to find a clearer example of the dangers in naïvely transplanting scientific concepts to the realm of social practice.

One irony is that Professor Skinner himself, after claiming teaching machines to be an 'application of basic science' (p. 397), admits in the next breath that current machines might have been designed on the basis of classroom experience and common sense, and are even explainable in traditional terms. This admission not only seems to remove the presumed evidential ground for the immediately preceding claim, but serves also to puncture the scientizing in Lane's review.

Skinner's paper, though more moderate than Lane's review, is, unfortunately, not at all clearer on the topic of values. He also is apparently not satisfied with what man has been, and wants to find out what he may become 'under carefully controlled conditions,' but he states further that '*the goal of education should be nothing short of the fullest possible development of the human organism*' (p. 398, my italics). (As a technology, education is still immature, he says, because it defines its goals in terms of traditional achievements and is concerned with reproducing the characteristics of already educated men.) It is not clear if the above-stated value judgment is thought by Skinner to be a consequence of the 'science of behavior,' nor if, alternatively, he takes it to have some independent warrant. At any rate, Skinner does not appear troubled by the fact that 'the fullest possible development of the human organism' is not merely a vague but a virtually *empty* prescription for education, because there is no *single* fullest possible development of the human organism: *conflicting* possibilities exist with qualitatively different characteristics; educational theory *starts* from this fact. Unless we indicate what *purposes* are projected, what *direction* we shall follow in developing human possibilities, we shall be in danger of rushing headlong in all directions, or finding ourselves on a path we never properly evaluated. Without such indication of purpose, the ideal of the *new man* is no ideal at all, but only a morally dangerous facsimile.

But aside from values, Skinner's and related systems seem to me to court conceptual confusion by trying to encompass everything. So Lane, in the passage earlier quoted, assumed that all educational goals would turn out to be 'desired behaviors,' apparently without pondering the conceptual absurdity of construing as *behaviors* such goals as individuality, imagination, integrity, autonomy, and sensitivity. And Professor Skinner, too, seems determined to fit everything in, including, along with 'simple verbal repertoires,' also thinking, and even the solution of personal problems. Is it a wonder that the analysis of thinking turns up such things as 'attending' (to what? how? to what purpose?) and 'studying' (involving taking notes, outlining,

constructing mnemonic patterns, and other 'behaviors which...
are of more subtle dimensions')?

To be sure, Skinner admits that much remains to be done in
analyzing scientific and mathematical thought, but says there is
no reason to suppose it less adaptable to programmed instruction
than simple verbal repertoires, once the behavior is specified. No
differences are acknowledged between simple tasks governed by
mechanical routines and creative theoretical constructions. All
are specifiable and all programmable. Old-fashioned inductivism
in the philosophy of science and discredited cookbook approaches
to science education are apparently here put together in the nut-
shell of behaviorism.

Certain general difficulties in Skinner's approach have been
pointed out by Scriven and by Chomsky, and I am not concerned
to discuss these issues here. Rather, I want to show how behaviorism functions as *educational theory* in Skinner's hands. Put
briefly, his claim is that the new behavioral analysis is superior
to traditional notions of knowledge and ability. The educator is
led to believe that there is something suspect in all those aspects
of education which cannot be exhaustively analyzed into overt
physical movements or complexes of such. On the other hand,
when the claim of behavioral superiority is put to the test of
critical examination, a curious result emerges: the claim turns
out to be *empty*, since behavioral notions are no narrower or less
abstract than the traditional ones, which, in any event, are admittedly indispensable. Thus, the plausibility of behaviorism (in the
present context) derives from its disguised duplication of
traditional ideas, while its radical shock value and narrowing educational effect derive from its spurious claim of
superiority.

I take one example from Skinner's paper. He writes,

> We can define terms like 'information,' 'knowledge,' and 'verbal
> ability' by reference to the behavior from which we infer
> their presence. *We may then teach the behavior directly* ...
> Instead of teaching an 'ability to read' we may set up the
> behavioral repertoire which distinguishes the child who knows
> how to read from one who does not (p. 383).

Now, obviously, if the behavior is simply a *sign* or *inferential
base* for determining the presence of knowledge, and (as appears
from the last quoted sentence) the behavioral description is not
equivalent to its traditional counterpart, then 'behavior' will *not*
suffice to *define* 'knowledge' and the latter term is therefore not

eliminable behaviorally. But perhaps there is at least a *practical* advance, in that the behavioral base is clearer than the vague notion of 'knowing'; surely the appropriate behavioral repertoire is more determinate than the vague concept 'knows how to read.'

First, however, Skinner substitutes for 'knows how to read' the concept *'shows* he knows how to read,' offering to analyze the *latter* behaviorally. Then, he says the latter in fact involves a behavioral repertoire of great complexity, of which he gives several *examples*, ending with *'and so on, in a long list'* (p. 383). Where is the advance over the original, 'traditional' notion? Did anyone 'traditionally' ever deny that *showing one knows how to read* may be indicated by the cited examples, i.e., reading aloud, finding objects described in a text, *etc., in a long list?* Did anyone ever have trouble 'traditionally' in applying this notion? Conversely, does it help in any way to sharpen the 'traditional' notion to be given several such examples, and then told there is a very complex behavioral substitute, *which is not further specified nor defined?*

Professor Skinner suggests that, because it is a large task to get a child to acquire the elements of the behavioral repertoire associated with reading, 'it is tempting to try to circumvent it by teaching something called "an ability to read" from which all these specific behaviors will flow' (p. 384). Presumably, it is better to say we are teaching or 'setting up' *a behavioral repertoire* from which they will flow. Or (perhaps), far better to say we are teaching items belonging to a *behavioral repertoire,* than items belonging to an *ability.* Behavioral terminology is after all scientific; it *must* be superior to traditional terminology. How far are we at this point from word-magic?

Let us by all means advance the study of teaching machines and programmed instruction. Before we offer any technical rationale as an educational theory, however, let us be sure *at least to acknowledge* the relevant logical, philosophical, and educational issues.

Notes

1 B. F. Skinner, 'Why We Need Teaching Machines,' *Harvard Educational Review*, XXXI (Fall, 1961), pp. 377-98; and Harlan Lane, 'Review of *Teaching Machines and Programmed Learning,* by A. A. Lumsdaine and Robert Glaser,' *ibid.*, 469-76.

2 See, for example, N. Chomsky in *Language* (1959), Vol. 35, pp. 26-58, and M. Scriven, 'A Study of Radical Behaviorism' in *Minnesota Studies in the Philosophy of Science*, Vol. 1, Minneapolis: University of Minnesota Press, 1956.

Reflections on Ryle's theory of knowledge

15

Introduction

The Concept of Mind, by Gilbert Ryle,[1] is one of the most in-fluential and important works in recent philosophy. Since its appearance in 1949, its theses have been elaborated, defended, assumed, and rebutted in countless publications. Its style of argu-ment has colored the thinking of a whole generation of philo-sophers. Its broad range of topics and rich treasury of examples have enabled it to serve as a common resource for inquiries vary-ing widely in direction, motivation, and presupposition. It has, in short, earned for itself the status of a modern philosophical classic.

Offering a many-faceted theory of the mind and its functions, it does not, however, purport to 'increase what we know about minds, but to rectify the logical geography of the knowledge we already possess' (p. 7). It is Ryle's thesis that

> during the three centuries of the epoch of natural science the logical categories in terms of which the concepts of mental powers and operations have been co-ordinated have been wrongly selected. Descartes left as one of his main philosophical legacies a myth which continues to distort the continental geography of the subject (p. 8).

This myth, which Ryle refers to as 'the dogma of the Ghost in the Machine,' is, in his view, not simply a collection of particu-lar mistakes, but one big mistake of a special kind, namely, *a category mistake*. 'It represents the facts of mental life as if they belonged to one logical type of category ... when they actually belong to another' (p. 16).

Slightly expanded version of a paper that appeared under the title, 'On Ryle's Theory of Propositional Knowledge,' *Journal of Philosophy*, Vol. LXV (1968), 725-32; reprinted by permission of the publisher. A preliminary version was presented at the Spring 1968 meetings of the Middle Atlantic States Philosophy of Education Society.

Ryle's general strategy in refuting Descartes is to account for intelligent conduct by looking to the behavioral patterns and dispositions in which it is embedded. Concerned, in particular, to emancipate intelligent performance from dependence upon the apprehension of truths, *The Concept of Mind* naturally places greater stress upon *knowing how* than upon *knowing that*. I want here to reconsider its treatment of the latter. I shall argue, first, that this treatment is inconsistent and, second, that certain remedies suggested by selected passages in the book are untenable.

Knowing as an achievement

Ryle is concerned with the proper categorization of mental powers and operations. How do we determine, however, to what category a thing properly belongs? Ryle offers no general account, but provides a well-known series of illustrations of category mistakes (p. 16). His guiding principle seems to be that things belonging to the same category should be subject to the same sorts of qualification, and accessible also to the same sorts of question. In particular, if something is an activity or performance, it should be capable of the same sorts of modification and accessible to the type of questioning normally applicable to activities or performances. Application of this principle leads to a denial that *knowing that* is an activity. To suppose it an activity is, indeed, a category mistake. How, alternatively, should *knowing that* be construed?

In certain important passages (pp. 130, 150-1) Ryle presents a general distinction between task verbs and achievement verbs. The failure to distinguish between them leads to dire epistemological consequences. 'Special cognitive acts and operations have been postulated to answer to' achievement words 'as if to describe a person as looking and seeing were like describing him as walking and humming instead of being like describing him as angling and catching, or searching and finding' (p. 151). Furthermore, since knowing is not qualifiable by adverbs such as 'erroneously' or 'incorrectly,' if it is further construed as an operation or performance, it seems to follow that there is some cognitive performance immune to mistake. Ryle writes,

> It has long been realized that verbs like 'know,' 'discover,' 'solve,' 'prove,' 'perceive,' 'see,' and 'observe' ... are in an important way incapable of being qualified by adverbs like

'erroneously' and 'incorrectly.' Automatically construing these and kindred verbs as standing for special kinds of operations or experiences, some epistemologists have felt themselves obliged to postulate that people possess certain special inquiry procedures in following which they are subject to no risk of error... So men are sometimes infallible (p. 152).

The fact that doctors cannot cure unsuccessfully does not mean that they are infallible doctors; it only means that there is a contradiction in saying that a treatment which has succeeded has not succeeded (p. 238).

The conclusion is, then, that knowing is not a mode of inquiry any more than curing is a mode of treatment. There is no more reason to suppose there is some infallible investigative procedure than there is to suppose that there is some medical strategy which never fails. Inquiry is a matter of our efforts to attain knowledge, whereas knowledge requires the satisfaction of independent conditions holding as a matter of fact. It is 'the distinction between task verbs and achievement verbs' that here 'frees us from ... [a] theoretical nuisance' (p. 152). The upshot of Ryle's discussion in these passages, then, is that *knowing that* is an achievement.[2] Let us now, however, turn to another theme of Ryle's general account.

Knowing as a capacity

A fundamental contrast that runs through *The Concept of Mind* is that of dispositions and occurrences. Occurrences are concrete events, happenings, or episodes, whereas dispositions are latent properties, abstract sets, potentialities, habits, tendencies, or capacities (p. 116). Now a major division among dispositions is that separating capacities from tendencies. Attribution of a tendency tells us that something will very likely be the case, whereas attribution of a capacity denies the likelihood that something will not be the case. As Ryle puts it, ' "Fido tends to howl when the moon shines" says more than "it is not true that if the moon shines, Fido is silent." It licenses the hearer not only not to rely on his silence, but positively to expect barking' (p. 131).

In a very important later passage, Ryle declares that 'know' is a capacity verb, 'signifying that the person described can bring things off, or get things right,' whereas ' "believe" ... is a tendency verb and one which does not connote that anything is brought off or got right' (pp. 133-4). He is clearly referring, in this passage, to *knowing that* rather than *knowing how* and affirms explicitly that *knowing that* and *believing that* operate in the same field and have propositional significance. Yet he declares that 'to know is to be equipped to get something right and not to tend to act or react in certain manners.' His reason for the distinction is that belief 'can be qualified by such adjectives as "obstinate," "wavering," "unswerving,"' etc., whereas knowing cannot. But it is not at all clear that the distinction he offers in explanation can be coherently maintained.

He declares belief to consist in propensities 'to make certain theoretical moves but also to make certain executive and imaginative moves, as well as to have certain feelings' (p. 135), illustrating the point by elaborating the variety of responses to which someone is prone if he believes that the ice is thin; e.g., he tells others the ice is thin, he skates warily, he imagines possible disasters, and so forth. But what of the person who *knows* the ice is thin: does he not share the same propensities? Ryle admits that, 'A person who knows that the ice is thin, and also cares whether it is thin or thick, will, of course, be apt to act and react in these ways too' (p. 135). He argues, however, that to say someone keeps to the edge because he *knows* the ice is thin is to employ a different sense of 'because' from that used in saying he keeps to the edge because he *believes* the ice is thin. To which one might reply that this latter consideration is quite beside the point. It is not the sense of 'because' that is in question but rather the interpretation of knowledge as capacity: if *knowing that* involves the same *tendencies or propensities* as believing, how can it be contrasted so sharply with believing, as belonging to the category of *capacities*? Moreover, it is generally held that to *know that* something is the case implies to *believe that* it is; on general grounds, one would then suppose *knowing that* to involve whatever attributions are accomplished by *believing that*.

These considerations show that there is at least a problem of interpretation for Ryle on this point. Possibly, there is some way of meeting it. It might, perhaps, be suggested that knowing, unlike believing, does not consist *solely* in propensities, but comprises also a surplus of capacities. It is questionable whether this suggestion is likely to provide an adequate solution, but I shall not argue the point here, since, in any event, a much more serious difficulty looms: capacities and propensities are *both* dispositional, and it is inconsistent to offer any sort of *dispositional* account of knowing and also to consider knowing an achievement. To this fundamental difficulty I now turn.

Achievement versus capacity

Ryle, as we have seen, considers *knowing that* an achievement. He also considers it to be dispositional. The trouble is that these properties exclude each other, so the joint attribution is self-contradictory. For Ryle explicitly introduces his main discussion of achievement words (pp. 149-53) by stressing their episodic character, i.e., their character as signifying occurrences, while he stresses equally that dispositional statements 'narrate no incidents' (p. 125), holding that to classify a word as dispositional is to say at least 'that it is not used for an episode' (p. 116). Nor does he ever suggest that 'know' is a hybrid word which is both episodic and dispositional, of the sort he talks about under the label of 'semi-hypothetical' or 'mongrel categorical' statements. He is perfectly clear and explicit in classifying 'know' as a dispositional word, without qualification (p. 116). He is also perfectly straightforward in calling achievement words 'genuine episodic words' (p. 149). It follows that 'know' cannot be both an achievement word and a dispositional word. Ryle's total account is thus literally inconsistent.

In *Conditions of Knowledge*, I erroneously suggested (pp. 26-28) that Ryle's notion of achievement led to a conception of knowing as an abstract *state*. In this I was misled by my own view that belief is, roughly speaking, a state that aims at the truth, while knowing succeeds in this aim (p. 25), knowing constituting an achievement state relative to belief. Further, my primary motivation was to discuss Ryle's argument against infallibility, an argument that does not peculiarly depend upon an episodic conception of achievement. So I did not sufficiently clearly distinguish my own abstract notion of achievement from Ryle's episodic notion. Ryle does, however, imply clearly that knowing is episodic, that (barring lucky achievements) it consists in the performance of a bit of inquiry with a certain upshot. Unfortunately, as we have seen, he also says that knowing is dispositional, hence not episodic at all. This is the inconsistency I promised to show.

Capacity for achievement

Are there any remedies for Ryle's predicament? A first proposal that suggests itself immediately is almost as immediately seen to be inadequate. Of achievements Ryle says in one of the places

above noted, 'They are not acts, exertions, operations or performances, but ... the fact that certain acts, operations, exertions or
performances have had certain results' (p. 151). Perhaps, then,
an achievement should thus be literally identified with the *fact
that* an act has had some result, in which case it will no longer
be episodic, since *facts* are not episodes or occurrences but
abstract entities presumed to correspond with truths. But if
achievements are thus abstract, there is no longer any incompatibility in holding knowing to be both achievement and disposition, inasmuch as both are properly conceived as nonepisodic.
To this proposal it may be objected that, though facts and dispositions are both nonepisodic, it does not follow that knowing
or anything else can be coherently construed as both a fact and a
disposition. Dispositions are, if anything, properties: to ascribe
a disposition to *x* is to attribute to *x* a property. *That x has a
certain property* may be a fact, but it is not in turn another
attributable property. Conversely, to say it is a fact is to hold
that a sentence asserting that *x* has this property is true; but to
say that smoking or knowing is a disposition makes no analogous
appeal to truth, for there is no corresponding sentence that is even
a candidate for truth.

The passage we are here concerned with runs counter to the
preponderance of Ryle's statements on the subject, in which he
forthrightly declares the episodic nature of achievements; in fact
he explicitly treats achievement words as a class of performance
words. 'Many of the performance-verbs with which we describe
people,' he writes, '... signify the occurrence not just of actions
but of suitable or correct actions. They signify achievements'
(p. 130). I conclude that the first remedy rests on a loose statement
of the episodic theory and does not, moreover, offer a viable
alternative.

A second suggestion relates to the fact that the acquisition of
a capacity is itself governed by criteria. A capacity may be learned
gradually through performance, and will be judged to have been
acquired only when some stipulated standard has been met.
Thus, to *have* a learned capacity is to have achieved success in
meeting a relevant standard of performance. Knowing, as a
capacity, in this way represents also an achievement. This idea
is, in itself, reasonable enough in the case of *knowing how*, but
it is not at all evident in the case of *knowing that*. Standards are
certainly relevant in the latter case as in the former, but it is not
clear that they involve *performance* in both cases, nor, *a fortiori*,
a gradual refinement of performance. Practice is not directly
relevant to propositional knowledge as distinct from skills; a

boy may practice swimming, but not knowing that 3 and 5 make 8.[3] Nor, if he knows he has a headache, has he had to master some ingredient evidential procedure for determining that he has a headache. To be sure, it may be argued, he has had to acquire language, but this is a general precondition for all, or almost all, cases of propositional knowledge, and something more distinctive seems to be indicated, something that relates to the access of the particular competence and not to past occurrences thought necessary for all. Finally, this proposal lacks specificity: what sort of capacity is knowing, if it is a capacity? What does it enable the knower to do?

Ryle himself suggests an answer to this question which gives rise to a third proposal. For he speaks of knowing as a capacity to 'bring things off, or get things right' (p. 133). The element of achievement suggested here is that which forms, so to speak, the *object of* the capacity. It is what is *enabled by* acquiring the capacity, rather than located in the antecedent process through which the capacity may have been acquired. This process, where it has occurred, has been adjudged successful only because the capacity that is its outcome is thought to facilitate or enable an independent and distinctive form of achievement.

We have here the kernel of a third proposal which seems much closer to Ryle's intent. This proposal is to construe knowing not as itself an achievement but rather as a capacity *for* achievement. The proposal thus classifies knowing as dispositional and remains thus inconsistent with those passages which treat knowing as itself an achievement. But it is nevertheless suggested in certain sentences of Ryle's discussion. It is, further, a natural proposal in the sense that it enables us to understand the source of Ryle's difficulty: starting with the idea of episodic achievements, he glides easily to the more abstract notion of the capacity for such achievements, without marking the transition. So in saying that knowing is an achievement, he is really to be interpreted more accurately as intending to say it is a capacity for achievement.

The suggestion receives further support from the following passages: (1) Just after describing achievement words as signifying that a performance has been carried through successfully, Ryle says, 'Now successes are sometimes due to luck... But when we say of a person that he can bring off things of a certain sort ... we mean that he can be relied on to succeed reasonably often even without the aid of luck' (p. 130). He thus shifts from considering the *single actual occurrence* of a successful performance to considering the *capacity* to carry out successful performances of analogous kind.

(2) On the same page he writes:

> When we use, as we often do use, the phrase 'can tell' as a paraphrase of 'know,' we mean by 'tell,' 'tell correctly.' We do not say that a child can tell the time, when all that he does is deliver random time-of-day statements, but only when he regularly reports the time of day in conformity with the position of the hands of the clock, or with the position of the sun, whatever these positions may be (p. 130).

The latter passage suggests paraphrasing 'know' as 'can tell.' If we can assume that the suggestion applies to *knowing that* (rather than, or as well as, to *knowing how*) we have a proposal to construe propositional knowing as a capacity to perform successfully in certain ways, namely, in telling correctly or truly. Each instance of correct telling is an episode classifiable as an achievement, strictly speaking. Knowing is not to be identified with any such instance, however. Rather, it is the *capacity* to generate instances of this sort. Does this idea, however, provide an adequate conception of propositional knowledge?

Discovering and saying

We must begin our examination by noting an ambiguity in the verb 'tell.' Sometimes it means 'say' and sometimes 'discover.' We might be tempted to rule out the latter meaning immediately, for, while we can speak of 'saying correctly,' we cannot speak of 'discovering correctly.' Nevertheless, Ryle suggests treating inquiry procedures as forming a 'subservient task activity' for knowing. Let us then first consider knowing as a capacity for discovery, in the sense of inquiring successfully. Each instance of finding out is an achievement, strictly speaking, whereas knowing is the general capacity to find out.

This proposal does not, upon reflection, seem to me to be tenable. We all know many things that we lack the capacity to have found out. A boy may know the Pythagorean theorem in the sense that he can understand it and grasp its proof; yet he may not have had the capacity to discover it, nor need he now have the capacity to discover analogous theorems. (And what is the relevant notion of a class of analogous theorems, anyway?) Conversely, a person may have the capacity to find out what time it is, without knowing what time it is. A person may not know the car is in the garage, but he certainly could not therefore be said to lack the requisite inquiry procedure for determining that it is or is not.

Let us then turn to the other meaning of 'tell,' i.e., 'say.' John has the capacity to say truly that it is three o'clock if and only if he knows that it is three o'clock. This proposal also seems to me untenable. For what interpretation shall we put on the capacity to say truly? Suppose John believes it is two o'clock, because his watch has stopped, whereas it *really is* three o'clock. Does he lack the capacity to say 'three o'clock' and to say it, therefore, truly? If he knows English and has no speech impediments, he surely can say 'three o'clock.' Yet he does not believe it is three o'clock and therefore clearly does not know this. If he is taught a theory or told a story that is in fact true, he may well have not only the capacity but even the tendency to repeat it under suitable classroom circumstances and thus to 'tell correctly'; yet he may not accept the theory or story, and, not believing it, cannot be said to know it. This version of the present proposal thus seems to me also to fail.

I cannot here enter into a consideration of alternative views, beyond noting the position taken in *Conditions of Knowledge*, that 'knowing appears to resemble rather those things that fit the categories of attainment, attitude, or, most broadly, *state*' (pp. 27-8). I do hold that propositional knowledge involves a state of belief as well as some independent factual condition truly described by the belief in question. Such knowledge is not, in my view, a performance, nor is it even a capacity, at least in any direct and straightforward sense of this term. It is independent of discovery and certainly of linguistic response. Yet it involves all of these, in complex ways. That is to say, it qualifies performance, presupposes and modifies capacity, is partly evidenced in discovery, and influences utterance. Like theoretical entities in science, it is deeply and widely linked in an explanatory way with observational phenomena and low-level dispositional traits. Yet, like such entities, it is not reducible to phenomena and dispositions, characterizing, in independent and complex ways that are as yet problematic, 'the orientation of the person in the world.'[4]

Notes

1 Gilbert Ryle, *The Concept of Mind*, London: Hutchinson; New York: Barnes & Noble, 1949.

2 Ryle's general contrast between tasks and achievements is criticized

on independent grounds in my *Conditions of Knowledge*, Chicago: Scott, Foresman, 1965, pp. 31-3.

3 For related points, see Jane Roland Martin, 'On the Reduction of "Knowing That" to "Knowing How,"' in B. Othanel Smith and Robert H. Ennis, eds, *Language and Concepts in Education.* Chicago: Rand McNally, 1961, pp. 59-71. This is a revised version of her article which appeared first in *Philosophical Review*, LXVII, 3 (July, 1958), pp. 379-88.

4 *Conditions of Knowledge*, p. 90.

16

The practical as a focus for curriculum: Reflections on Schwab's view

In a pair of provocative and searching studies, Professor Joseph J. Schwab has set forth a critique of the prevalent state of curriculum thinking and proposed a fundamental reorientation of such thinking from a theoretical to a practical emphasis.[1] 'The field of curriculum,' in Schwab's view, 'is moribund. It is unable, by its present methods and principles, to continue its work and contribute significantly to the advancement of education. It requires new principles which will generate a new view of the character and variety of its problems.'[2] I want, in the present paper, to offer a critical account of some of Schwab's basic ideas, which seem to me intrinsically interesting and, moreover, important for education.

Introduction

The sorry state of the curriculum field has, in Schwab's opinion, come about because of an 'inveterate, unexamined, and mistaken reliance on theory.' Theories have been freely borrowed from outside the field of education and put to use in the attempt to 'deduce' aims and methods for schools; moreover, the effort has been made to construct theories of curriculum and instruction. But 'theory, by its very character, does not and cannot take account of all the matters which are crucial to questions of what, who, and how to teach.' Many of the borrowed theories are incomplete even as respects their own subject matters. Finally,

A preliminary version presented in Jerusalem, in September 1971, at a Curriculum Conference sponsored by the John Dewey School of Education of the Hebrew University and the Jerusalem Van Leer Foundation. The present version of the paper was given at a Harvard seminar, in February 1972. Thanks are due to the University of Chicago Press for permission to quote from *School Review*, Joseph J. Schwab, 'The Practical: Arts of Eclectic,' Vol. 79, 1971; and to National Education Association for extracts from *The Practical: A Language for Curriculum*, Schwab, 1970.

'even where a borrowed theory is adequate to its own subject matter, it begs or ignores questions about other subject matters.'[3]

What is wanted, according to Schwab, is a shift from the theoretical to the *practical*, the *quasi-practical*, and the *eclectic* modes.[4] Whereas the theoretical is directed toward the search for general knowledge, the *practical* is directed toward decision, a decision having 'no great durability or extensive application' but applying 'unequivocally only to the case for which it was sought.'[5] Theoretical inquiry proceeds under control by a principle that determines the character of the problem, the relevant data, and the canons of evidential interpretation.[6] On the other hand, the practical is not rule-governed in the same way, since practical problems 'arise from states of affairs which are marked out by fulfilled needs and satisfied desires as being states which do not satisfy, which hurt us, or which deprive us of more than they confer.'[7] Practical problems require identification, but such identification does not proceed by rule. We need to find out what it is we want or need and also what part of the state of affairs it is that requires changing.

> These matters begin to emerge only as we examine the situation which seems to be wrong and begin to look, necessarily at random, for what is the matter. The problem slowly emerges, then, as we search for data, and conversely, the search for data is only gradually given direction by the slow formation of the problem.[8]

The method of the practical, which Schwab calls 'deliberation,' is, as he explains it, 'not at all a linear affair proceeding step-by-step, but rather a complex, fluid, transactional discipline aimed at identification of the desirable and at either attainment of the desired or at alteration of desires.'[9]

In the *quasi-practical* mode, we have an extension of practical deliberation to problems confronting systems with internal diversity.

> What is required is that the deliberations narrowly proper to each organ of the system ... be carried on in part with the help and advice of able representatives of the other organs involved. Deliberation about the physics course requires the comment of the English teacher as well as the teacher of biology, the learning theorist as well as the science educator.[10]

In participating in quasi-practical deliberations, each person will typically need to learn new vocabularies and to come to appreciate considerations hitherto regarded by him as 'alien and irrelevant.' He acquires through participation 'an additional sense of proprietorship' in the problems of relevant agencies other than his own. He also needs to learn to honor delegated powers, that is, to recognize that 'the ultimate practical decision ... must be taken by the organ which the problem most concerns.'[11]

The *eclectic* mode is concerned with overcoming the weaknesses of theory in order to render theory useful in practical application. Eclectic arts help us to 'ready theory for practical use. They are arts by which we discover and take practical account of the distortions and limited perspective which a theory imposes on its subject.'[12] Eclectic arts aim to reveal the particular limitations of any given theory and to join different theories in order to form a more appropriate tool for application to problems of practice. Education, in particular, is a matter of complexly related actions forming a

> skein of myriad threads which know no boundaries separating,
> say, economics from politics or sociology from psychology...
> Yet our fullest and most reliable knowledge of these matters is
> not knowledge of the web as a whole. It is knowledge of
> various shreds and sections of the whole, each shred and
> section out of connection with other shreds and sections. It is
> the knowledge conferred upon us by the various behavioral
> sciences. Some six sciences are involved: a kind of behavioral
> epistemology, concerned with what men know or can find out;
> a kind of behavioral ethics, concerned with what men
> need and want and what among these wants and needs
> conduce to a satisfying life; sociology-anthropology; economics;
> political science; and psychology.[13]

These sciences are not likely to be theoretically unified. 'What is required is a practical healing, a recourse to temporary and tentative bridges built between useful parts of bodies of knowledge in the course of their application to practical problems.'[14]

In a discussion of the teaching of eclectic, Schwab considers how to make 'the riches of the radical pluralism of theory ... accessible to educators in training.'[15] His discussion is too elaborate to summarize here, but he hopes that students will come to appreciate the variant resources and limitations of different applicable theories, and achieve facility in employing such theories serially or conjointly in dealing with the particulars of a practical problem. He proposes a training method in which each theory of a given set is brought to bear on cases in such a way as to be transformed 'from a doctrine to a *view*, from a body of "knowledge" to a *habit* of observation, selection and interpretation of the appropriate facts of concrete cases.'[16] One theory after another of the set in question is treated in such a way as to bring out the 'plausibility'[17] of its assumptions and to turn it into a 'lens'[18] for viewing the facts under a special perspective. Cumulative treatment enables the comparison of variant theoretical assumptions as well, and may encourage a capacity for the intelligent use of multiple perspectives in dealing with new problems of practice.

The import of these ideas for education generally is expressed by Professor Seymour Fox, a student and collaborator of Schwab, as follows: 'The eclectic ... constitutes one protection against the many "band-wagons" we have suffered from in education,' in which curricular decisions have been made and acted upon under the guidance of a single theoretical apparatus, in isolation from other legitimate perspectives. These several perspectives

> offer an exciting challenge to the educator to create the richest eclectic combination of theories that complement the one under consideration. But no matter how ... rich and valid our eclectic combinations, it is to the more difficult and artistic task of deliberation that the bulk of our curricular efforts will fall... Deliberation has as its goal the development of specific materials and strategies for their introduction into the school system after they have been experimented with and refined in the educational reality.[19]

The above sketch of Schwab's ideas does not do justice to the detail of his treatment, in the course of which various theoretical and practical issues are analyzed and numerous educational observations, of considerable interest, are offered. Nevertheless, his main points are, I believe, now evident and I turn thus to the critical consideration of their import, adding further detail as the need may arise in the sequel.

First, I should express my agreement with much of what Schwab has to say on the topic of curriculum. Surely the state of the field is vulnerable to the criticisms he offers. In particular, we have indeed had a series of blithe theoretical intrusions from psychology and the social sciences, each over-confident, each relatively blind to the contributions available from other quarters, each relatively insensitive to the rich body of experience embodied in the lore of educational practice, each acknowledging only reluctantly the autonomy of practical criteria, and the relevance of such criteria in assessing educational programs as well as in providing critical, if partial, tests of guiding theoretical approaches. Surely the independence and dignity of educational practice need to be reaffirmed; such practice needs to be rediscovered not only as a source of human wisdom but as a locus of cognitive import, illuminated by theory and, in its turn, illuminating theory.

Moreover, I agree that it is important to stress *application* as a field worthy of study. Philosophy—even the philosophy of science—has tended to restrict itself to analysis of the content, structure, and import of theories taken as statements within well-defined disciplines; it has, furthermore, emphasized the role of fundamental theories in the most advanced sciences. I agree that *theoretical application* needs itself to be studied systematically and seriously, that soft as well as hard sciences deserve attention, that applied as well as pure sciences require study and that the arts of practice and the processes of practical judgment merit sustained and detailed investigation.

Finally, I applaud the stress on the diversity of theoretical viewpoints in dealing with problems of practice, and the emphasis on interaction and mutual accommodation in fitting theory to case. The notion that one can confidently proceed by simple deduction from theory to practical recommendation without regard to related theories, auxiliary assumptions, or possible feedback from recalcitrant cases into the theoretical assumptions themselves, is certainly a mistaken notion. As William James put it,

> you make a great, a very great mistake, if you think that psychology, being the science of the mind's laws, is something from which you can deduce definite programmes and schemes and methods of instruction for immediate schoolroom use. Psychology is a science, and teaching is an art; and sciences never generate arts directly out of themselves. An intermediary inventive mind must make the application, by using its originality.[20]

To explore the details of application through which inventive minds may exercise their originality is an important task, and Schwab's exploration of certain of these details represents a significant contribution to this task.

Having indicated a broad area of agreement, I proceed now

to formulate certain criticisms and reservations concerning basic features of Schwab's analyses. My critical remarks will be grouped under five headings: 'Scientific theory and educational theory,' 'The theoretic versus the practical,' 'Incompleteness, partiality and distortion,' 'Theoretical difference and theoretical conflict,' and 'Appreciation and criticism.'

Scientific theory and educational theory

Schwab's discussion centers on scientific theories, mainly on theories drawn from psychology and the social sciences. His characterizations of theory are especially appropriate to theoretical examples belonging to the empirical sciences. In referring to educational problems, he says that our fullest and most reliable knowledge of these matters is given by six behavioral sciences: behavioral epistemology, behavioral ethics, sociology-anthropology, economics, political science, and psychology. This list is striking in its omission of humanistic studies and in the consequent suggestion that behavioral science is, in general, more trustworthy or pertinent than the humanities. I find it, however, impossible to believe that behavioral epistemology is superior to epistemology, that behavioral ethics is more reliable than ethics, or that sociology is fuller or more illuminating than history. Moreover, ethical, epistemological, and metaphysical assumptions have certainly entered into the belief systems with which theorists have approached educational practice and, reliable or not, such assumptions seem to be inescapable ingredients of such systems. Furthermore, historical interpretations of the social contexts of educational institutions have played a significant role in forming the beliefs and attitudes determinative of educational practice.

The omission in question strikes me as doubly ironic. In the first place, it is out of tune with the major emphasis on diversity, which is a strong point of Schwab's analysis. In the second place, it excludes *such analysis itself* and others like it, which seem to me clearly philosophical rather than behavioral-scientific in character. The cluster of doctrines that bear on educational practice is certainly a composite of diverse ingredients, and there seems to be no good reason to exclude all but the scientific contributions.

I suspect that despite Schwab's admirable critique of the 'corruption of education' by the narrow application of scientific theories,[21] his analysis may still be dominated by a scientific conception of theory. In a certain respect his view may be compared to that of D. J. O'Connor, who, in a book published some years ago, deplored the fact that educational thought falls short of the rigorous criteria of scientific theory.[22] Schwab, of course, takes the contrary position that educational thought ought not to be theoretical but rather practical since, as he says, the 'theoretic bent has let education down.'[23] But he seems to share O'Connor's implicit notion that *theory* is to be taken always or ideally as *scientific theory*, and it is this notion that prepares the way for the omission noted above.

One can remedy the omission simply by adopting a more comprehensive conception of *theory*. An alternative and, in my opinion, preferable remedy is suggested by the approach of P. H. Hirst.[24] Hirst argues that there is a legitimate and familiar sense of 'theory' in which what is referred to is not scientific theory but the composite set of beliefs that serves to organize and guide a given realm of practice. In this sense, the concept of *educational theory* is perfectly legitimate, but such theory is not to be confused with scientific theory; it is composed of diverse elements, and it includes philosophical and normative components, in particular. In this respect it resembles rather social theory and political theory than scientific theory. The advantage of such a construction is that it recognizes not only the relative independence of practical thought but the full diversity of contributions to such thought. In particular, it recognizes the relevance of general doctrines of a philosophical and ethical character to educational theory, thus preventing a monopoly of *theory* by the scientists. Theory, in a word, is too important to be left to the scientific theorists.

The theoretic versus the practical

Schwab asserts 'the radical difference of the practical from the theoretic mode.'[25] This sharp *opposition* is in striking contrast to the emphasis he places on *continuities* between means and ends in the process of deliberation. In any case, I believe that the opposition in question is too sharply drawn—that it cannot really be maintained in its present form.

What are the bases of this opposition? The end of the theoretic is general knowledge, that of the practical is 'a decision, a selection and guide to possible action. Decisions are never true or trustworthy.' They can be judged only comparatively, and apply clearly only to the single case.

> The subject matter of the theoretic is always something taken to be universal or extensive ... the subject matter of the practical ... is always something taken as concrete and particular ... this student, in that school, on the South Side of Columbus, with Principal Jones during the present mayoralty of Ed Tweed and in view of the probability of his reelection.[26]

Theory, we are told, achieves its character, 'its very generality,' by abstraction from particulars, whereas 'the practical is ineluctably concrete and particular';[27] indeed, it consists of the 'particulars from which theory abstracts.'[28]

Now take first the idea that the theoretic mode aims at knowledge whereas the practical aims at 'a decision, a selection and guide to possible action.' It seems to me a rather restricted view that takes decision as a *guide* to action and sees it as the end of practical thought. Decision, it might be argued, is itself, as distinct from its expression in words, a *form of* action rather than a *guide to* action. Whether or not this argument be judged compelling, however, it must be admitted that we seek guidance in *making decisions* themselves. Such guidance cannot consist in further, *anterior* decisions without infinite regress. In fact, I believe it consists in statements with prescriptive force, *expressing* decisions and contextually implying the existence of good reasons for them, embodied in principles of action of varying generality, supplemented with information of relevant sorts.

Moreover, statements of decision themselves vary in generality: the line between general decisions and principles is not a sharp or theoretically important one. Practical thought attempts to answer such questions as 'How shall I act?' 'What should be done?' 'What course of action ought to be followed?' etc. The answers to such questions are not decisions; they are *answers* and, as such, they *can* be appraised, indeed, they invite appraisal as good or bad, trustworthy or not, by reference to the context of relevant practical principles and presupposed information. Indeed there are thinkers who hold that moral principles are to be appraised also as true or false. At any rate, it is clear that the aim of practical thought is not only the implementation, or even the expression, of specific decisions, but the formulation of more general intentions and prescriptions, embracing *practical and moral* principles. Such expressions and formulations guide decision, and thereby, action.

If we clearly distinguish, at any rate, between a practical principle and the particular decision of an agent applying it, the contrast in generality as between the theoretical and the practical fails to emerge. For a principle *must* be general: it must impose a structure of classes of actions, and reasons appropriate to them. That principles may change is nothing to the point: theories may change as well. That principles guide particular and unique decisions is irrelevant, since theories guide the analysis of particular and unique empirical situations.

Indeed, in speaking of 'a practical mode,' we are, I believe, committed to *generality*. A *mode* of thinking must, whether it concerns natural facts or human decisions, employ rules, methods, principles, standards, criteria. To say that 'the practical is ineluctably concrete and particular' is at best to describe not the *mode* itself but the cases taken as its objects. In this event, however, one might with equal justice say that the reality investigated by science is ineluctably concrete and particular.

Is there not, however, a contrast to be made with respect to abstraction? Do we not confront the given case in its full particularity in deciding how to deal with it, whereas the theorist needs rather to abstract from its particularity in constructing his theories? I believe this contrast is also exaggerated. It neglects the fact that particulars are *described* and that *description in itself* is abstractive. To speak of 'this student in that school, on the South Side of Columbus, with Principal Jones during the present mayoralty of Ed Tweed and in view of the probability of his reelection' is to impose a variety of descriptive categories which are abstractive and selective *as descriptions*. Theory makes further abstractions, it may be conceded, but the difference is relative at best. We never cope with the full particularity of an object or situation. What could such coping imply: taking account of all its properties? Such a conception is, I believe, impossible. Our thought is, whether general or particular, always abstractive, always selective. In bringing theories into co-ordination with particulars, we never escape the necessity of abstraction—we never grasp reality in its totality and immediacy. To sum up, I agree that a distinction can be drawn between theoretical and practical modes of thought. But I hold that all thinking is abstractive and employs generalities. Practical thinking is concerned with the guidance of action; but the expressions and formulations in which it issues are to be distinguished from the actual decisions or actions guided by them. These expressions and formulations may, and normally do, draw upon a wide variety of parent sources in the scientific and humanistic fields.

Incompleteness, partiality, and distortion

If abstraction is a necessity of thought, it is inappropriate to call abstraction a 'vice' of theory.[29] In the first place, it is inconceivable that there *could* be a theory which did not abstract. In the second place, abstraction is not in any case peculiar to theory. Even when we bring theory into connection with particulars, our apprehension of the latter proceeds under certain aspects, rubrics, categories, or concepts. Thus if abstraction is a vice of theory, it is no less a vice of any form of thought, inclusive of the practical.

Moreover, Schwab seems to me to be in danger of taking the *incompleteness or partiality* of a theory in itself to be a sign of its falsification of reality. Thus, he speaks of the 'violence' that a theory does to its 'chosen subject in order to disconnect it from related subjects and give it the appearance of an independent whole.'[30] Coupled with his notion that even the best theories are 'radically incomplete,'[31] the doctrine that abstraction is a vice and that theories do violence to their subjects seems to court a general skepticism or mysticism: if discursive thought is inevitably a distortion of reality, we ought never to trust it, or we ought to trust rather some form of direct encounter with reality, via intuition.

Schwab, to be sure, takes rather the line that distortions can be overcome by supplementation; the distortions of different theories being, so to speak, cancelled out through their joint use. But this does not seem to me a sufficient remedy. A long abstraction is no less abstract than a short one. No matter how many theories are put in combination, they will still, in their totality, fall short of absolute completeness through omitting infinitely many features of the relevant particulars of their subject matter. A more inclusive theory may deal with more features than a less inclusive theory, but each will be infinitely partial, hence infinitely incomplete, and therefore infinitely distorting of reality.

Now I reject the notion that theoretical incompleteness falsifies reality. Moreover, I do not believe that Schwab's theory of eclectic indeed requires the general concepts of incompleteness and distortion that I have been criticizing. If *completeness* of a theory is logically impossible in the sense under consideration, there is no point in calling theories *incomplete*. If abstraction is logically necessary, how can it be thought a vice? If all thought is couched in, and is therefore relative to, a system of concepts or a language, truth and falsehood must themselves be so relativized.

It is, after all, abstract statements in particular languages that are true or false; the fact that a statement cannot simultaneously express *all possible* truths does not detract from it own truth. A theory does no *violence* to its subject if it is true, but its truth is certainly a particular truth, expressed by statements of the theory, in the language appropriate to it. There is no way of overcoming its 'radical incompleteness' if by that we mean its character as an abstractive unit of thought. But there may still be the best of reasons in the world for combining it with other theories, and assumptions of other kinds, in mounting an attack upon a given problem of explanation or practice. Comparative completeness, if understood not as a feature related to abstraction, but rather as a *relative* property varying with the particular *problem*, may still be a useful notion: in solving a specified *problem*, that is, a given set of statements may be more adequate than another. Such a problem-relative notion of comparative completeness, without any implication of *distortion* or falsification of reality, is fully adequate, I suggest, to motivate the study of eclectic arts that Schwab has developed.

Theoretical difference and theoretical conflict

Schwab's emphasis on the plurality of theories available is of the first importance, in my opinion. From the point of view of application to practice or indeed of explanation, the available plurality simply provides greater resources than are offered by any single theory. Problems of explanation, prediction, and control, as they arise in life, are surely not guaranteed to fall within the range of any single scientific discipline, much less any single theory. How could they be? The intellectual divisions between disciplines and theories cannot be taken as indicating metaphysical rifts in nature; they are rather fluid separations of convenience, altering with the course of ongoing investigations. In approaching problems of explanation, interpretation, and action, we ought surely to be ready to bring to bear the totality of our intellectual resources, at least in principle, and to override academic, disciplinary, and traditional divisions.

The notion of plurality has, however, a further significance, from the point of view of theoretical *evaluation*. For it embraces not only the concept of *different* theories, but also that of *competing or conflicting* theories. Plurality is, in itself, utterly neutral as between theories that *differ* and those that *conflict*. But the latter distinction is of crucial significance from the standpoint of theoretical evaluation. That is to say, theories that are in logical conflict cannot both be true. One or the other, or both, must be surrendered, or—if the conflict depends upon some common auxiliary premiss—that premiss may be yielded instead. In any case, the theoretical situation needs reevaluation, and measures must be taken to avoid the acceptance of a contradiction. There can be no tolerance of contradiction, for if you are willing to accept a contradiction, you must be willing to accept anything; and the whole concept of a *systematic framework*, which *excludes* as well as *includes* statements of relevant sorts, is, in effect, surrendered.

Now there is a sort of pragmatic rivalry which may characterize *logically compatible* theories, *relative to a given problem*, where the question is which theory will provide a more satisfactory solution of that problem. But the issue I am concerned with is not such merely pragmatic rivalry but genuine logical contradiction. To be sure, when we set about using accepted theories in *application* to problems of explanation or action, we presume such theories to be compatible, and we ought to be prepared to combine them relevantly so as to effect solutions maximally adequate to these problems. However, the critical evaluative attitude ought never to be wholly suspended during the process of application. Such a process may itself bring to light hitherto unnoticed incompatibilities of a decisive logical sort. The presumption of logical compatibility may itself, that is, be challenged and, indeed, overridden, with a consequent need to reappraise our initial theoretical equipment. Faced with the spectre of contradiction, we can no longer take a sophisticated attitude tolerant of diverse but partial viewpoints.

I fear that these considerations, though they are perhaps likely to be acknowledged by Mr Schwab, are not made explicit in his analysis. Indeed, the whole major emphasis of this analysis is on ways of supplementing and joining several individually partial and incomplete theories for a more adequate attack on given problems, and such supplementation presupposes that these theories are at least logically compatible. 'Eclectic operations,' he writes, 'permit the serial utilization or even the conjoint utilization of two or more theories on practical problems.'[32] In other passages, however, he occasionally refers to the theories in question not merely as presenting different partial views, but as *competing*. 'The eclectic,' he writes, 'may concern itself with *competing* theories of one or similar subject matters...,' and the knowledge yielded by eclectic 'makes it possible to apply different *competing* theories *appropriately* to different practical problems.'[33] Supplementation, I submit, is not a proper response to incompatible theories.

In one passage, after remarking on the inadequacies of several curriculum recommendations, he seems to blur the critical distinction by suggesting that these recommendations 'need to be joined and reconciled.'[34] Joining, I suggest, is appropriate where the elements are logically compatible; reconciliation is appropriate only where they conflict, and reconciliation precludes joining—it requires revision somewhere in the premisses generating conflict.

In offering his proposals on the teaching of eclectic, Schwab remarks that

> students might begin to discern the fact that the members of
> a plurality of theories are not so much *equally* right and
> *equally* deserving of respect, as right in different ways about
> different kinds of answers to different questions about the
> subject and deserving different respects for the different
> insights they are able to afford us.

Different views of literature might be discovered to be 'not contradictories, one or both of which must be wrong, but contrarieties, different facets differently viewed, each of which is *some* part of the whole.'[35] Granted that such a discovery *may* sometimes occur, and granted that *when* it occurs it may be extremely significant, does it always need to occur? Can we say that all members of *any* given plurality are right in different respects, each offering a view of some part of the whole? I cannot see the necessity of such a universal claim. The notion that all theories are partial does not imply that they are all compatible. The idea that partiality inevitably distorts, which we discussed and criticized earlier, may lead to a fundamental skepticism about all discursive thought. It may, on the other hand, lead to an attitude of overtolerance: if every theory is bound to distort, we ought to lower our sights and incorporate all the partial views in a charitable spirit. Both attitudes are, I believe, mistaken. Partiality does not inevitably distort. Partial views may be inconsistent with one another. And a partial theory may be utterly wrong. Neither total skepticism nor total charity is a reasonable attitude, in the face of such considerations.

Appreciation and criticism

If it is true that theories may be logically incompatible, and that any given theory may be wrong; if it is further true that the critical-evaluative attitude ought not to be totally suspended even during processes of application; then, it seems to me, students ought to be educated not merely *to appreciate* the resources of compatible pluralities of theory but also *to be critically alert* to conflicts and to other failures of theory. It seems to me that the latter aim is not adequately represented in the remarks of Schwab on the teaching of eclectic.

He is concerned to foster the mastery and utilization of theoretical pluralities—to encourage sophistication, flexibility, and facility of thought in applying theories to practical problems. While I applaud this aim and recognize the propriety of its emphasis in certain phases of the training of educators, I think that it can never be wholly sundered from the aim of fostering critical attitudes. The two aims may, certainly, generate a certain psychological tension between them, but I believe that educators need to seek some optimum balance incorporating both, rather than choosing one or the other, even in a restricted form of training.

Schwab's scheme for the teaching of eclectic apparently presupposes the exclusion of *poor* theories at the start. These, he says, 'can be identified and eliminated by various familiar methods of analysis and criticism and are, in the course of the history of most fields of enquiry, in fact eliminated.'[36] Now, in the first place, it seems to me important, even if such elimination can be relied upon as a historical fact, to train students in the requisite critical methods appropriate to such elimination. In the second place, Schwab characterizes these poor theories as the vague, ambiguous, trivial, and unsupported, speculative theories. The remainder he considers 'good theories,' and it seems to me beyond question that good theories, so construed, may still turn out to clash with experience or with one another. The fact that they *are* good, in Schwab's sense, does not mean that they can be taken utterly for granted. Alertness to the possibility of their failures needs, I should think, to be encouraged and sustained.

Schwab's purpose is to transform 'a doctrine to a view,' 'a body of "knowledge" to a *habit* of observation, selection, and interpretation of the appropriate facts of concrete cases.' He speaks of each view as a 'lens' through which the facts are to be seen. He deplores as a 'very common and most pathetic student response' to a multiplicity of theories the query, 'Which one is right?'[37] A more adequate response, from Schwab's point of view, is an appreciation of the 'plausibility' of the assumptions of each theory.[38] The students are no longer to ask their 'sometimes brazen, sometimes simple and unembarrassed, sometimes shy and troubled'[39] query, 'Which one is right?' but to learn to see the variety of perspectives available for interpretation of the same data and to appreciate the differing explanatory resources of each.

Now it seems to me that plausibility is a very poor guide in matters of theoretical evaluation. I agree with Karl Popper's view that almost any theory, indeed even vague, ambiguous, trivial and speculative theories, can appear plausible, for even such theories can be shown to comprehend a variety of cases as positive instances. The critical question is not whether they can be shown plausible, but rather whether they can be shown to be falsifiable, that is, subject to negative tests.[40] Plausible theories may be not only falsifiable, but false. To work through the details of a theoretical construction to determine how it may be put to the test is not incompatible with appreciating its plausibility. It is a further task, without which it seems to me that a proper grasp of the claims of a scientific theory cannot be attained. To stop short of training for this task seems to me inadequate, even if the main goal is mastery of techniques of application.

It may certainly happen, to be sure, that two theories are evenly balanced or virtually evenly balanced, so that the question, 'Which one is right?' has no answer under the circumstances. Even this judgment, however, requires a basis not simply in the *plausibility* of each theory but in a detailed comparison with respect to their capacity to deal with actual and potential counter-cases. Moreover, it is certainly true, I believe, that *not every* two theories of a given domain *are* evenly balanced and that in such cases the student's query *does* have a definite answer, even if provisional and relative to the data at hand. The student's query is therefore, I believe, a healthy and important one, for it acknowledges the seriousness of theory as making a claim to truth. It is, presumptively at least, always in order, though it does not always have a definite answer. It cannot, therefore, be appropriate to reject it in favor of a sophisticated grasp of alternative views. The aim of sophistication is not, I am convinced, in conflict with the aim of critical judgment. Both need to be fostered together.

The practical as a focus for curriculum

I wish to conclude this essay by reaffirming my agreement with many of Schwab's conceptions, and expressing the hope that the foregoing criticisms may be helpful in the further elaboration of these conceptions. The problems he has addressed are surely of great importance to education, and their continued investigation will be likely to benefit both theory and practice.

Notes

1 Joseph J. Schwab, *The Practical : A Language for Curriculum*, Washington, D.C.: National Education Association, 1970; and Joseph J. Schwab, 'The Practical : Arts of Eclectic,' *School Review*, 79 (1971), 493-542. The first of these publications will be referred to hereafter as *PLC*, and the second as *PAE*.

2 *PLC*, p. 1.

3 *PLC*, pp. 1-2.

4 *PLC*, p. 2.

5 *PLC*, pp. 2-3.

6 *PLC*, pp. 3-4.

7 *PLC*, p. 3.

8 *PLC*, p. 4.

9 *PLC*, p. 5.

10 *PLC*, p. 9.

11 *PLC*, pp. 9-10.

12 *PAE*, p. 495.

13 *PAE*, p. 501.

14 *PAE*, p. 502.

15 *PAE*, p. 506.

16 *PAE*, p. 519.

17 *PAE*, pp. 522, 526.

18 *PAE*, p. 516.

19 Seymour Fox, 'A Practical Image of the Practical,' address delivered to American Educational Research Association convention, Feb. 1971; mimeograph, pp. 2-4. In *Curriculum Theory Network*, 1972.

20 William James, *Talks to Teachers*, New York: Norton, 1958, pp. 23-4. These talks were first delivered in 1892.

21 See Joseph J. Schwab, 'On the Corruption of Education by Psychology,' *Ethics* 68 (1957), 39-44; also *School Review* 66 (1958), 169-84.

22 D. J. O'Connor, *An Introduction to the Philosophy of Education*, New York: Philosophical Library, Chap. 5.

23 *PAE*, p. 493.

24 Paul H. Hirst, 'Philosophy and Educational Theory,' *British Journal of Educational Studies*, XII (1963), 51-64.

25 *PLC*, p. 2.

26 *PLC*, p. 3.
27 *PAE*, p. 494.
28 *PAE*, p. 496.
29 *PLC*, p. 25.
30 *PLC*, p. 14.
31 *PAE*, p. 505.
32 *PLC*, p. 12.
33 *PLC*, p. 13.
34 *PAE*, p. 500.
35 *PAE*, p. 512.
36 *PAE*, p. 505.
37 *PAE*, p. 507.
38 *PAE*, p. 522.
39 *PAE*, p. 507.
40 Karl R. Popper, *The Logic of Scientific Discovery*, London:
    Hutchinson, 1959, and *The Open Society and Its Enemies*,
    Routledge & Kegan Paul, 1945.

Index